# Money Talks

# Money Talk$

## The Leader's Guide to Finance Conversations

*(even if you hate numbers)*

Matthew Needham

Published by Matthew Needham Consulting Pty Ltd



Cover design and typeset by BookPOD
Printed and bound in Australia by BookPOD

ISBN: 978-1-7643228-0-5 (paperback)
eISBN: 978-1-7643228-1-2 (ebook)

NATIONAL LIBRARY OF AUSTRALIA
A catalogue record for this book is available from the National Library of Australia

*To Emma and Sam xx*

*And to every leader who finds finance boring.*
*You're the reason I wrote this.*

# Contents

INTRODUCTION

# The Financial Literacy Gap

*Most people don't hate finance – they hate feeling stupid.*

There I was in a meeting room looking over Wellington Harbour on one of those rare, late spring mornings when the wind takes a break and the sun actually shows up. Seated in front of me was a man with responsibility for allocating billions of dollars of public money. That's the GDP of a small country. Or a house in Sydney with parking.

By the time he finished talking, the penny had dropped. I finally saw, right in front of me, plain as day, the biggest thing that was getting in the way for everyone.

But let me back up a moment. A good story deserves a bit of context.

Prior to the meeting with Mr Billions, I had been consulting with a government agency. I'll leave the details out (no one likes a tittle-tattle), but, to give you a sense of what we were working with, his operation was responsible for spending billions of dollars a year.

We're talking big money, big impact, complex issues and political undercurrents through it all. And right at the centre of all this was this particular leader. For now, let's call him John.

John was a lawyer by trade, senior executive by title. The sort of leader you'd trust in a crisis — he'd land the plane, organise getting the passengers out, and have a press release and ministerial briefing drafted before the wheels touched the ground.

We'd crossed paths before in bigger meetings, but this was our first proper sit-down conversation. I really wanted to get a good understanding of what each part of the organisation did to figure out how I could help the finance team become more influential.

In the first 30 minutes, everything I guessed about John — sharp, insightful, totally in command of the issues — was proven right. I was nodding along, pretending to keep up, while he guided me through the complex responsibilities of his area as if he were talking about last night's All Blacks game.

So far, so good.

Then I asked him: "Do you have any feedback for me on the Finance team?"

Immediately, something shifted.

That confident posture faltered as he paused, leaned back and crossed his legs, as if shielding himself from the conversation. The universal body language of someone about to say something they probably shouldn't.

A moment passed. Then another. At this point, I was starting to wonder if there was something big coming, some kind of difficult feedback that I'd have to work out how to explain to the Finance team. But I couldn't have been more off-target.

Silence.

Then, with a nervous laugh, he said: "Well, the thing is, Matthew, I find finance really boring. So I try to have as little to do with it as possible."

I wasn't expecting that.

Billions of dollars of financial responsibility ... and he avoids finance like a politician giving a straight answer.

Billions of dollars of financial responsibility ... and he avoids finance like a politician giving a straight answer.

I didn't say anything for a second or two, giving myself a moment to let it land. And to make sure I didn't burst out laughing, as I couldn't believe I was hearing this from a senior leader.

My first thought was: "That can't be right. Maybe I misheard." Followed quickly by: "No, that's what he said to the consultant."

Here was someone who was in charge of major budgets. His decisions didn't just impact the hundreds of people working for him in the agency —— they came with major implications for millions of New Zealanders! And more than that, this guy was so obviously competent, so expert in his area, but had obviously mentally filed "finance" under "not my problem".

How could he possibly be running things strategically if he didn't even pretend to care about the numbers happening in and around the policies he and his team were creating? I couldn't wrap my head around how to respond.

"I'm just not really a numbers guy," he followed up with a casual shrug.

And that's when it hit me. Despite the billions of dollars, he was responsible for, he just didn't see finance as part of his role. He didn't consider financial matters, happenings or decisions as something that had much at all to do with his area, his decisions or his orbit within the organisation.

Over the next few days, I reflected on other conversations with and about leaders I had encountered over my career. I remembered another CFO lamenting some years before at a finance conference about how the senior leaders in his organisation proudly wore "I don't do finance" and "I'm not a numbers guy" like medals on a general's uniform. Over time, I've realised that this perspective, this total aversion to all matters financial, is actually incredibly common among many leaders.

Now, whenever I run workshops with non-finance leaders I always start by asking: "Who hated maths at school?" Most of the leaders grin and raise their hands, while others look around nervously to see whether anyone else is raising their hand before raising theirs!

Throughout my professional life I have been mostly surrounded by finance and commercial professionals. And so until I worked in government, I hadn't truly understood how disliked (perhaps even feared and misunderstood) finance was to most leaders.

This led me to delve deeper into what was behind this common aversion to numbers and finance. And it got me thinking: If these leaders were able to overcome this blind spot around finance, *how much more could they be capable of?*

If non-financial leaders could have better conversations with their Finance teams about the performance of their area or organisation, what could that do to an organisation's results?

This book is the result of my work to answer that question — and my solution to this all-too-common problem for people who hate numbers and avoid finance.

## Why we need a better system for non-financial leaders

While we elevate good people to important roles with budget responsibilities, they often don't have the financial skills or awareness to actually make good decisions. Maybe we shouldn't be so surprised: after all, we want them in these roles for their leadership skills and technical knowledge, not because of their experience in managing budgets.

I've met countless brilliant leaders who feel completely lost when finance enters the conversation. They'll say "I don't do numbers." And yet understanding numbers — or, more accurately, knowing how to talk about them — is critical for their success as leaders. We know this. So then why do so many non-financial leaders keep coming to the table feeling like they want as little to do with numbers as possible?

It's not as though organisations are not keenly aware of the role financial savvy plays in their success. In fact, some organisations prioritise financial upskilling for their leaders; we all want our people across the executive table to understand finance and make better decisions

But what does that upskilling process actually look like? Usually it's courses, conferences, workshops and digital seminars. And a lot of businesses invest in financial awareness training, too.

But are off-the-peg, one-size-fits-all solutions the most effective approach? Sure, if someone were sufficiently interested in finance, then sending them on a course might be a good idea. But what about everyone else? Shipping off self-proclaimed numbers-haters to a finance course is a little like forcing someone who hates reading into a book club; it just exacerbates the gap between them and the excitement you wish they had.

So are there other ways of helping non-financial leaders thrive in their financial awareness without herding them off into 'remedial' programmes that just don't work? How do we help those who don't want to "Awaken their inner accountant", as the shout line for the Australian Institute of Company Directors' Finance for Directors course trumpets?

Well, that's what this book is for.

*Money Talks* is my guide for people who find finance really boring.

Chances are, that's you. Someone who doesn't have a finance background but regularly interacts with budgets, reports and finance teams, and wants to be a leader without having to also be an accountant.

But by the end of this, you're going to know how to have better conversations about finance so that you can make better decisions. And the best part? You don't have to learn about the numbers or accounting concepts.

This book definitely won't turn you into an accountant, and it won't replace your melatonin at night by lulling you to sleep with memorising financial terms and formulas. It's here to help you thrive in the workplace by showing how you can use your innate curiosity (and a healthy degree of scepticism) to ask insightful questions about your organisation's performance or the area under your control.

You need clarity. You need simplicity. You need repeatable frameworks. And you need results.

This book will give you the tools to find your way through financial conversations and budgets. I'll offer you simple frameworks that don't require poring over spreadsheets or getting into technical tangles with maths and equations. Instead, we'll focus on the story that numbers and finance tell us.

My hope is that by the end you'll feel well-equipped to start engaging in financial conversations with a bit more curiosity and confidence. And the result — for you and your organisation — will be stronger collaboration with your finance team and far better strategic decisions being made across the board.

## Why every leader can (and should!) engage with finance

Most people leave school hating maths. This is no secret. Believe it or not, I did, too; I'm fully aware of the dread most people feel when they see formulas and figures.

Learning maths can escalate from simple concepts to quadratic equations very quickly. My son is in his teens, and he's certainly in that maths-averse camp. "Why do I even need to know what a hypotenuse is, Dad?"

He raises a good point. Much of what we learn at school has little relevance to what we will need later in the outside world (unless, of course, you're going into one of those specific jobs that requires tricky maths). But we learn it anyway, because while not everyone is going to be a geographer or an historian or a triangle specialist, some of us will be. (If I had a dollar for every time I met one of those triangle specialists …)

And what happens is that those school leavers who don't end up going into a career that specifically uses maths enter the workforce still hating and resenting it. They thank God that they've got that all mathematical muddling behind them, and can safely consign it, along with their school uniform, to a motley if nostalgic past, sure in the belief that it is hard work and doing well that will see them promoted in the working world they are now launching into.

And sure, this might work for a few years. They go about their business, they get better at what they do. But then — lo and behold — they get to a certain level of leadership and what happens? Budgets, data, numbers, projections, formulas. They've come up against maths again.

Like a pin popping a balloon, that excitement at getting their first management position rapidly dissipates when they are confronted by some helpful person from Finance, asking them to confirm a monthly budget or forecast. All that euphoria over the new job or promotion is instantly replaced with a sense of profound dread: they're going to have to deal with numbers.

Invariably, the numbers you've probably come across in your role have to do with money — budgeting, allocating costs, interest rates. And as you become more senior, finance becomes an ever-increasing part of the job. If it's not finance, other numbers-based measures like visitor numbers, click-through rates, net promoter scores, units sold, students enrolled, lifetime customer values, and conversion rates will occupy increasing amounts of your time and attention.

And it's hardly surprising that dealing with numbers brings out beads of cold sweat for many people. The hangover from this all-too-familiar number panic is often tied up with feelings of inadequacy which lead to shame, secrecy and feelings of being judged. Especially if you're a high-performer. I've seen this in those leaders who deal with finance by blocking it out. For those staunch "I don't do numbers" leaders, ignoring numbers is a way of dealing with that shame stemming from struggling with hateful maths at school. But this shame is more than a lingering unpleasant memory of the past; it is also a barrier to current learning — one that can lead to poor decision-making, with significant implications for your organisation and potentially your career.

Vulnerability in financial conversations can generate *curiosity*, which can be a real asset in a world where default assumptions of certainty can too often hold sway.

The good news, though, is that uncertainty around maths and finance doesn't have to be a weakness. In fact, I've seen first-hand that coming to finance as a non-numbers person can actually become a superpower. As Brené Brown tells us in *Rising Strong*: "Vulnerability is not weakness; it's our most accurate measure of courage."

Vulnerability in financial conversations can generate *curiosity*, which can be a real asset in a world where default assumptions of certainty can too often hold sway. The trick is not to feel like you have to learn everything there is to know about finance (after all, that's the Finance team's job), but instead to learn how to have better awareness, focus and conversations with your Finance team

— on your terms, and to help your insight. In this way finance is not an end in itself, but a tool with which you can achieve and maximise your own wider objectives.

## The case for numbers

Understanding how numbers work — and how they can be misused — is one of the most important lessons you can learn in life, not just as a leader.

Numbers are often used to support a point of view. They seem to be presented as incontrovertible facts, when in reality they are frequently present only part of the picture, being one-sided, biased and designed to manipulate. So, when looking at any presentation of numbers a healthy dose of scepticism goes a long way — and helps you make the right decisions.

Case in point: In *Calling Bullshit*,[1] Carl Bergstrom and Jevin West discuss how tobacco companies have historically used misleading statistics to downplay the dangers of smoking. A tobacco company may claim that only 0.2% of Americans died of cancer in 2022, and this is factually correct. But presenting the number of deaths from smoking-related cancers as a percentage of the total population — rather than of the absolute number of deaths — makes it look less significant. Cancer accounted for 20% of all deaths among Americans — around 600,000 deaths out of a total of 3.2 million deaths in the same year. As Bergstrom and West say, percentages can be a powerful way of disguising bullshit.

If you don't know how to interpret numbers — and the words around them — then you are susceptible to being misled.

You're going to miss important things, and potentially make misinformed decisions.

Graphs can also be used to deceive and mislead, even when they're purportedly showing "just numbers". A good example of this was exposed by Marc Lallanilla, writing in *Live Science* about a graph purportedly showing a decline in gun-related murders in Florida following the "Stand Your Ground" gun-law change.[2]

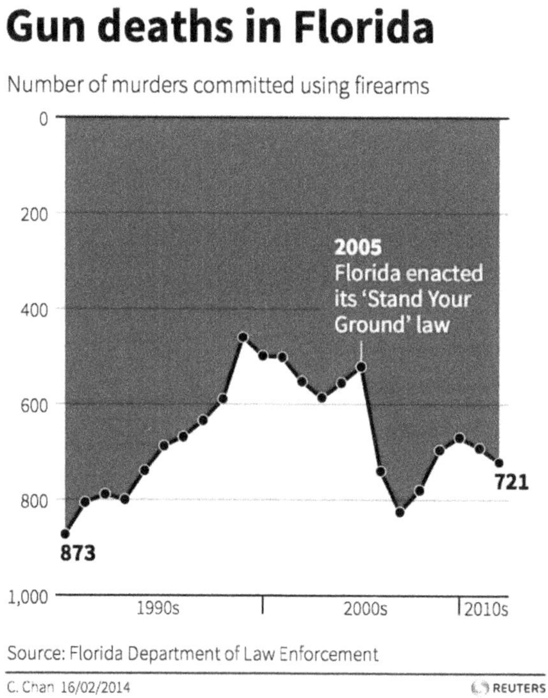


At first glance, the graph looks as though the 2005 gun-law change has resulted in a decline in gun deaths in Florida, as the tracking line peaks midway in the period under study, and then is on a downward trajectory. But look more closely and you'll see that the graph has been presented in such a way that it flips our usual perspective: the vertical axis has been inverted, with high numbers at the bottom and zero at the top. This means that if we glance at the image unquestioningly, chances are we will automatically assume that numbers increase as they go up the graph and decline as they go down, which is the usual way numbers are presented. So when we observe the numbers going in a downwards direction we will effectively "see" what we expect to see — a decline — and mistakenly conclude that the number of deaths is declining. However, if we approach the graph with curiosity and scepticism, and look a little more closely and critically, we will realise that the numbers have effectively been flipped, at which point it becomes clear that the "Stand Your Ground" law has corresponded with an *increase* in deaths, not a reduction.

Graphs can also be used to deceive and mislead, even when they're purportedly showing "just numbers".

Political campaigns are also rife with misleading graphs. A good example is given by Dan Satherley when he deconstructs a 2019 New Zealand National Party graphic in an article in *Stuff*.[3] It purportedly shows the cost of fuel under the Labour Government to be $2.23 a litre versus $1.91 a litre under the previous National Government.

Again, on the surface we might perceive this to be accurate and true. However, the visual representation is not an accurate depiction of the underlying data. For while the difference between $1.91 and $2.23 is just over 16%, the bar on the right is wider and taller (61% taller), thus making the tax difference appear much greater than it is. It seems like two-thirds of the cost of fuel under Labour is due to tax, when it is actually 50% versus 45% under National. What's more, National's bar depicts an average price over nine years (2008–2017), whereas the bar for Labour reflects the price on a single day (in 2019), which may even be unusually high — hardly a fair comparison.

It doesn't matter whether it's pie charts, scatter plots, tables, percentages, or numbers slipped into a speech: manipulating data and information in these ways can easily create a false impression and lead the recipient to draw incorrect conclusions. And it's easy to make the wrong decision when you don't really understand what you're being told.

With all of this in mind, it's easy to just get someone else to look at the numbers and interpret them for you — like members of your Finance team. But therein lies another challenge: Finance teams speak a different language. Thanks to their jargon and way of answering questions — even when you thought you understood the answer — sometimes you're still left confused! You start learning that 'it depends' means that the answer could differ every time you ask the question "Why are our travel expenses up?"

A former boss once said to me: "I'm sure every time I ask about whether we can capitalise something, I feel like the answer changes."

"It does," I replied, "because the context is always different."

When talking finance, this means that even terms you do understand can take on new meanings. So while "end of year" or "year-end" means 31 December to most people, it could actually be any date in the calendar depending on your organisation's financial year (many organisations follow the tax year which is the 1 July to 30 June in Australia, and 1st April to 31 March in New Zealand). What's more, to a budget holder, it's an artificial period, entirely abstract from what you do on a day-to-day basis, purely carved up for reporting or funding purposes.

Finance teams talk numbers all day long, and if you don't then it can feel like you might as well be speaking Spanish and trying to ask for directions from a French person to a restaurant on the other side of Paris. Sure, you could adopt the stereotypical tourist approach — speaking ever louder and more slowly — but, let's face it, that's not going to make you or the other person more understood. And it will lead to a frustrating conversation for both involved!

Miscommunications and misalignments happen all the time between Finance and other departments. For example, I recently worked with a Finance team that received feedback from stakeholders that budget owners were finding it difficult to authorise third-party payments because they could not know for certain that the payments were accurate. The Finance team was adamant that the budget holders were just being lazy. But once we dived in a little deeper, we saw something else happening: budget holders were being asked to authorise reimbursements for spending that they had no oversight or control over! The whole system was designed in an ineffective way. But both 'sides' had jumped to the conclusion that it was somehow the other party at fault for the messy situation.

Failing to understand each other is a big issue. Think of *Money Talks* as your Rosetta Stone or your Lonely Planet guide to your organisation's finances. Just like your phrase- or guidebook does not aim to turn you into a native speaker, *Money Talks* isn't about making you a financial guru. Instead, we'll focus on how you can get a clear enough understanding of the language and mindset of Finance teams so that you can start working together more effectively.

## What's at stake

In 2018 Carillion PLC, a British multinational construction and facilities management company based in the UK, collapsed owing £7 billion in debt. At the time it employed 43,000 people, 19,000 of whom were based in the UK. Over 30,000 suppliers and subcontractors were also affected, and Carillion, being one of the largest suppliers to the UK public sector, had 450 contracts underway at the time of its collapse.

Almost overnight, 2,500 jobs were lost. More than £150 million in supplier invoices were left unpaid, leaving thousands of subcontractors financially exposed. Multiple hospital and school building projects were delayed, and the insolvency process ultimately cost the UK taxpayer an estimated £148 million. A UK Parliamentary Joint Committee report on the collapse concluded that Carillion's business model was an "unsustainable dash for cash". The board was described as being both responsible and culpable for the company's failure.

It was a similar story for Australian electronics retailer Dick Smith, which collapsed in 2016 with debts of approximately A$400 million. Around 3,300 employees lost their jobs, and some A$23 million worth of gift cards and deposits were lost. Once again, the official report noted that, alongside a poor performance during the critical Christmas 2015 trading period, the business had expanded too quickly, with unsustainable increases in inventory that could not be converted to cash when needed.

What if the leaders in these organisations had asked better questions? What if board members or senior leaders at Dick

Smith were able to ask "What is our cash conversion cycle?" or "How many days' inventory are we holding, and is it sustainable?" And then critically evaluate and understand the answers they were given. What if they were able to flag risks much earlier?

If Carillion's leaders had asked "If we are doing so well, why do we need to take on so much debt?", then the collapse may have been avoided or at least better managed. The use of appropriate financial models, a clearer focus on early risk identification, and sharper financial questioning would have likely mitigated the scale of the financial crisis that followed.

All parties in an organisation, and their clients and subcontractors, need to have "money talks" — and to be speaking the same language when they do so.

I don't bring out these examples to shock or frighten you. In these cases, I'm sure the people involved were doing what they thought was the right thing to do. But the best intentions don't always lead to the best outcomes. For while it's easy to work out the questions to ask after the event, the reality is that good questions can only be asked and be effective when we fully understand the implications of the answers.

All parties in an organisation, and their clients and subcontractors, need to have "money talks" — and to be speaking the same language when they do so. This book aims to guide you through gaining a basic understanding of how finance works, and then give you frames and tools for better directing your energy and conversations. I'll give you questions to ask so that you can confidently unlock insights to help you make better decisions — ones that lead to better outcomes.

*All it requires is for you to be curious.*

*Money Talks* is designed to empower you with the knowledge and mindset to talk with your Finance team with confidence and clarity. It will help you foster a curiosity-driven approach to your learning and growth.

That's coming from someone who didn't set out to be an accountant. And yet understanding numbers — and communicating them better — has become my life. I went to university intending to study marketing and business, and ended up in accounting and finance instead. In the end, despite my deep dread, I found I really enjoyed the course. What interested me wasn't so much what we studied, but more the implications of how finance impacted an organisation. I suspect it also helped that I made some great mates and drank a lot of beer along the way ...

In my third year at university I had a placement working at Rolls-Royce, which led to an offer to join the Finance Graduate Programme when I graduated.

During my placement year I worked in Development Engineering, Manufacturing and Procurement Operations. My first project was to understand why so much of the engineering team's time (and cost) was being allocated to waste. (Inevitably it was due to the designers making errors in the drawings or changing their minds.)

I quickly came to understand that accounting was really about making things happen (or not happen) and making them better, and that is something I realised I have a real passion for. Accounting wasn't about counting things or reporting; it was about identifying and clarifying issues, understanding why things were the way they were, and then making decisions.

My accountancy career has taken me across the UK, Europe, the United States, Asia, New Zealand and now Australia, working in some of the world's largest organisations and running the largest sustainable financing programme in New Zealand. All the while, I've had a business-first mindset leading the way; I'm always seeking to improve the overall performance of an organisation. To me it has never been *all* about the numbers, but the way in which numbers keep the score and show us whether the organisation is on the right track.

## What's getting in the way? And what can we do about it?

So if we know that numbers are incredibly important indicators of whether the organisation is on the right track, what's stopping leaders from engaging in financial conversations?

Through the research, reflections and discussions I've had with leaders over the past couple of decades, I've identified three key barriers:

1. fear
2. lack of focus, and
3. friction.

### *Fear*

Type "What is the most hated subject at school" into a search engine (or survey almost anyone you know), and the top result will undoubtedly be mathematics. Even an article from June 1956 in *The New York Times* points to maths as being "the most hated subject", but also points out that maths is essential to develop scientists and engineers to compete with the Russians.[4] Seventy years later not much has changed.

For some people, a fear of numbers triggers similar responses to those people feel with other phobias like a fear of heights or spiders. Heart pounding, armpits sweating, rash emerging, breath shortening — sure seems fun, huh? In the case of numbers, this fear is called *numerophobia*.

Just as people with a fear of heights avoid climbing ladders or standing on balconies, people with a fear of numbers avoid conversations about numbers — even when having such conversations should clearly be a part of their job!

### *Lack of focus*

When presented with a spreadsheet and a sea of numbers and colours, most people don't know either what they are looking at or what to focus on. More experienced leaders often focus on what they know and then look for the biggest movement, but even doing that means that they could be focusing on the wrong thing.

In board meetings, with tight agendas and limited time allocated to discuss the finances, time spent focusing on the wrong thing chews up time, which could be more productively spent elsewhere.

What's more, if you're focusing on the wrong numbers when it comes to allocating resources for the business, you'll probably end up focusing those resources in the wrong place, too.

### *Friction*

How much easier does your life become when you ask the Finance team a question? If the answer is "not very", that's probably because there's some friction between your ability to ask questions of people with greater finance knowledge and their ability to answer said questions. In many cases, asking a simple question of Finance might leave you more confused than before you asked the question.

The result? Many leaders disengage from asking questions entirely. After all, who wants to risk not being able to understand the answer, or feeling like an idiot for asking a question that apparently everyone else already knows the answer to?

### *My approach to overcoming these barriers: The 3F framework*

Frame. Focus. Flow.

These three simple steps come together to form a framework for driving better financial awareness, stronger conversations with your Finance team, and (most importantly) better strategic decisions.

In this book, I'll walk you through each stage in detail. We'll develop a financial **Frame** using non-numbers-based models to help you paint a clearer picture of how your business and finances overlap and intertwine. Framing will give you an overview of how your strategy and your purpose can be better understood through financial information. From there, we'll look closely at how to **Focus** on the right things — the elements of your finances, metrics or measures of performance and information that will help you drive towards your goals. And finally, we'll look at how to **Flow** into action. This last section is about finding the right questions, methods and tools for engaging with your Finance team, having better conversations around finance, and ultimately working towards making better business decisions.

I've designed this framework especially for non-financial minds. It doesn't require any maths and it's easy to implement. By the time you get to the end of this book, you'll have everything you need to go through the framework on your own, in the context of your unique organisation, and use it to start collaborating with your Finance team in a more action-oriented way.

Now I'm sure you're just as excited as I am to get into this, but before we dive into the 3Fs, we have a bit of housekeeping to do first. There are a few terms, concepts and big-picture understandings that we need to get clear — I call these the financial basics. So, our first couple chapters will take you through what I see as our crash course on cash, cashflow and budgets for non-financial leaders. Once you're good and comfy with the language I'll be using for the rest of the book — and we're all on the same page with the basic function of financial systems — we'll be ready to dive into our trusty framework.

## How to use this book

When I was a kid, my mum told me I needed to look after books, respect them and not write in them, but this is your book and I'm not your mum. If underlining key points or putting notes in the margins helps you, knock yourself out. It's about you getting the best out of what works for you, not for someone else.

You can read this book cover-to-cover if you are interested in comprehensively understanding how better questions can apply to each area of managing your area's finances or making better decisions. Or you can dip in and grab an idea or two that you can use just before your next budget meeting. Or a combination of both. It's up to you.

All I ask is that you put your deep-seated fear of numbers aside and commit to being curious. Once you understand that our biggest opportunities may lie within our fears, you can start to look at fear differently, as something to be embraced rather than hidden from or ignored.

This book will help you reclaim your confidence in financial conversations, change your relationship with numbers, and unlock better answers. All so that your teams become aligned, resources flow where they're needed most, risks get spotted earlier, decisions become stronger, and outcomes improve.

Imagine a workplace where leaders and Finance teams collaborate instead of talking past each other. Where budgets aren't just spreadsheets, but maps that guide better strategy.

You don't need to master every number. But you do need to be willing to look beneath them — and ask the questions that bring you and Finance together, not drive you apart.

*Money Talks* will get you to that sweet spot. And for when you're there, I've created a set of practical tools to help you put these ideas to work straight away. Scan the QR code at the very end of this book, or head to **https://resources.matthewneedham.co/money-talks**, and you'll unlock companion worksheets, short videos and extra resources. Think of it as your backstage pass to the book: everything you need to turn these ideas into action in your next budget meeting (without needing a calculator).

But now, let's get started!

# PART ONE

# THE BASICS

*Finance doesn't happen in spreadsheets.*
*It happens in decisions*

## CHAPTER ONE

# The Basics

You already have the tools you need to have better financial conversations: basic numeracy and a curious mindset. That's it.

I've promised that this isn't a technical accounting textbook, and that's still true. To have better financial conversations, you don't need to know how to calculate EBITDA, run DCFs or understand your COGS. (Do you have the suspicion that they might recruit for accounting school just by asking who really loves acronyms?)

What you *do* need to know is how some of the core ideas fit together. So, think of this chapter as a chance to learn the rules of a game. While the only way to eventually get good is to play, before you dive in it helps to have a solid understanding of how the game functions at its core.

I want to do a few things in this chapter. First, I want to change how you think about budgets, then convince you that cash flow is the most important part of your organisation's ongoing success, and look at how cash appears in a financial report.[1] Once we've covered that, you'll be ready to look at how The 3 Fs model applies.

## Jam jars

As a budget holder, even a reluctant one, you probably think about budgets a lot.

Most people think a budget is about tracking your income and expenses. But a budget is so much more than that: it's your financial roadmap for executing your strategy. It is your plan for how resources will be allocated to bring your organisation's plans to life. By connecting day-to-day activities with your organisation's long-term goals, a well-constructed budget ensures that every dollar spent or received moves the organisation closer to achieving its vision. Just like moving your tokens around the board in a game of Monopoly! Hiring people or spending money on advertising? They are both part of delivering strategy, and so are tokens in achieving your end goal.

Most people think a budget is about tracking your income and expenses. But a budget is so much more than that: it's your financial roadmap for executing your strategy.

For example, when I became CFO of a social housing provider, the management report told me that we were spending much less on building new homes than we had planned. This meant we had much bigger cash balances than we had expected to have at that time of the year. The Finance team thought this was a good thing. However, unless we had suddenly found out how to build houses for much less than we had planned (which wasn't possible at the time), the cash surplus actually indicated that we were behind on building homes for vulnerable people. This left us in a tricky position: unless action was taken to increase building activity (and increase spending) we weren't going to achieve our strategy.

Boxing great Mike Tyson gives us a suitably pithy and memorable other way of looking at it: "Everyone has a plan until they get punched in the face."

A budget is your way of estimating and tracking how much money comes in and out of the organisation over a specific period (usually a year, but often also a quarter or a month). It's your blueprint or map for managing money effectively, and translates your organisation's strategic vision into actions.

A budget is intended to be the best estimate of what you plan to do over whatever planning period you're using (for example, a quarter, a year, three years, etc.).

You've probably heard a lot about budgets. They take up a lot of time in organisations. But here's a secret that Finance teams and senior leaders wouldn't like to admit: a budget is essentially *a guess*. A guess that's based on a set of assumptions. And the more assumptions you make, the more likely the budget is to be wrong. Investors or the board probably wouldn't be too impressed to receive a document for approval that was titled "Our best guess for the next 12 months". So, instead, we call it a budget, aka the *forecast*.

Once we have identified our end goal, we break it down into the sets of steps and tasks required to achieve it. We then allocate the resources needed to undertake these steps and tasks, and set up a set of timeframes in which each is to be achieved. This set of planning of resources, timeframes and identifiable markers of success together make up our budgeting and forecasting functions.

We tend to think of the budgeting function as allocating money to specific projects or expenses, like money set aside in jam jars.

As a young boy, I had a moneybox that was given to me by my sister, who adopted the jam jar principle. My moneybox sat on my windowsill. Anytime I came home with coins in my pocket or earned some pound notes, they'd go into one of a few different slots I had labelled on the moneybox. One slot was my budget for sweets and ice creams, so was labelled "treats".

I had another slot labelled "bike", so that I'd have savings set aside for when my bike's inner tubes inevitably burst or went flat. And yet another for books, movie tickets and CDs.

It's a good strategy for teaching kids about savings. And it's still how most people and businesses effectively think about budgeting today: putting aside certain amounts of money to cover different expenses or initiatives — training, stationery, building maintenance, rent, travel, and so on — and then spending that allocated money as it's needed.

Unfortunately, life does not appear to take too much notice of our jam jars and their respective levels of coinage! So what happens when I get lots of punctures in quick succession and I end up having to patch and replace my bike tyres so many times that I run the "bike" jar dry? I'd likely just take the cash out of another jar that had money in it. Or, alternatively, what if I don't plan on using my bike this year? Should I still set aside that bike-maintenance money, or just put it into the jar for movie tickets?

These unknowns of life, and the choices they throw our way, show that the jam jar analogy has real limitations — even though most businesses use more or less its equivalent to allocate and spend their budgets. What life's vagaries show us is that such a system is too rigid, too siloed. It treats each expense as separate from the others. It will also tend to make the budget holder feel guilty if circumstances change and budgets are used (or not used) in ways other than those planned in those best guesses. It also doesn't appreciate that all the aspects of a business — and therefore a budget — are interconnected.

I once worked at a university where the budget was strictly allocated: $10,000 for travel, $10,000 for training, $10,000 for stationery, and so on. On paper, it was a good control mechanism. Great, even: a clear line that we could track against. In practice, however, when one category went over budget people started charging those costs to other categories. When training actually needed $2,000 more, they would sneak it under the stationery budget. It was as if they were saying that they were buying comics, but were using the bike money to do it. It led to a lot of confusing accounting, requests for budget transfers, inaccurate reporting and bad decisions that not only make a nonsense of the year's budget, but ultimately did not help plan accurately for the next year's budget either.

When they'd look back, or a new manager took over, it would *seem* that their performance against budget was perfect, whereas in reality it was all held together with Band-Aids and sticky tape! They couldn't really see what was actually needed in each category, what was actually spent, or why. And the next year, when they did the same thing — $10,000 to each of those categories — they'd end up making the same mistakes.

So budgeting using the jam jar model promotes the wrong behaviour. Instead, we need to think about having buckets of jam instead of jars of jam: big preserving pans of bubbling jam, instead of dozens of individual jars. Buckets give you the ability to adjust as you need to. You might still plan on spending on CDs and movie tickets, but if you overspend on CDs, you can still cover the cost from within the entertainment budget.

It gives you flexibility and — even more importantly — accurate visibility.

What feels like a minor change to how you look at budgets is actually a massive change in mindset.

As I said at the start, your budget is a way of translating your strategy into actions. So instead of thinking about rigid categories, instead start with the questions: What do we need to do, and how much money do we need to deliver it? This will help you invest in the areas that matter most when it matters most. Because, as a budget holder, your job is to allocate resources in ways that either reduce friction or increase speed.

Maybe this year it's more valuable to invest in training instead of marketing. Maybe you're planning a push to a new market, in which case travel might take priority over stationery. You want to place the money where it makes the biggest impact in delivering your strategic vision, and invest accordingly. When you take on the bucket approach, you'll be able to allocate budgets with much more flexibility and simplicity when it comes time to review your next investments and spending.

It's important to recognise that sometimes, perhaps at a particular time of the invoicing cycle, your bucket might look like it's overflowing. At other times it might feel like you're scraping the bottom. That up-and-down can feel confusing. So let's explore what's happening with this movement — the changes of what's happening in your bucket. The term for this? Cash flow.

## Cash flow

The flow of cash is the single most important part of your business or organisation. This is true whether you're a conventional for-profit business, a not-for-profit business (sometimes called a 'for-purpose' or 'profit for purpose' business), or in the public sector. Because when you run out of cash, it's game over. You either go bust, or, if you're using public money, then you're breaking the law.

> The flow of cash is the single most important part of your business or organisation.

Think of it this way: Your business is like a water wheel. Water enters and turns the wheel, and some of it powers the system. Some gets lost or redirected. You need a minimum flow just to overcome internal friction and make the wheel turn. The goal is to keep the wheel turning efficiently, and extract as much power as possible from each turn of the wheel caused by the flow of water.

You want the flow of money coming in to be more than what you need to turn the wheel over, because then you can extract the most work from it. It's also helpful to redirect some water into a dam or a reservoir for when the river levels get low, keeping some aside for a dry period. I'd call it a rainy-day fund, but let's not mix our metaphors! Instead, let's call this your reserves.

Your business is the same. Money enters the business and powers business activity. Some gets used to pay staff, and to cover the other tools or processes that keep your business turning over. Some might spill over the sides; for example, faulty goods or services, or stock going out of date. You also want to build up a reserve to smooth over any interruptions to flow, or to deploy a larger amount all at once for bigger projects or investment. But, overall, the goal is the same: use the power of money to generate energy and momentum.

For a business, this 'water' is your cash. Run out of it, and the wheel stops. And if it stops, it might not start again. And that's why the heart of any good accounting conversation is understanding cash flow.

Cash flow conversations are some of the most important that you'll have as a budget holder, so it's important that you are familiar enough with the terms of the trade to ask good questions.

Let's look at how cash flows through a business, with an illustration that's far simpler than it at first looks. In the following text I will put some of the key terms in bold type, so you can easily link them back to where they appear on this little illustration to see how they fit together into the big picture.

In the middle, you have **cash,** the money that you have available for use. That cash comes from a variety of sources. If yours is a new business, it might be in the form of share capital or money introduced by the owner (like seed money). For more established businesses, it might be money you have left over in your accounts at the end of the financial year or it might come from borrowing money from others.

Let's say you did nothing with the cash — it would still be in your bank account, potentially gathering interest.

Businesses and organisations, of course, don't exist to just do nothing with that money, at least not if they're hoping to produce something or have some kind of impact. Instead, they spend that cash on various things to improve their operations or grow the organisation. They might invest in **assets** — those items that have a useful life to the organisation for longer than a year, like buildings, equipment and machinery — and which *could* be sold for cash. Organisations will also put money into **investments**, deploying cash into assets or projects with a view to getting future returns from them. And probably most importantly, they spend it on **stock** — all the inventory that they buy for resale. This counts towards the outgoings.

Money also has to go out to pay for **people** (your staff) and to pay any **expenses** (insurance, office rent, utilities and so on). That can include any expenses associated with having people in the business, such as employment costs, travel and training. Any of the money that the business has to pay for stock or other goods goes to the **suppliers**. Payments to suppliers cover not only materials you might need for producing whatever it is you are selling, but anything you might need to stay in business such as heating, lighting, subscriptions, etc.

Money comes in from **sales** of the **stock** or the services delivered by your **people**. If customers buy things off you on terms (e.g. they pay in 30 days' time) they are called **debtors** (customers who owe you money). Once these debtors have paid what they owe, this money gets added back to the **cash** pile again. That's the very basic function of a business and its money flow.

So far, so good. But most businesses also have other aspects affecting the inflow of money. **Share capital** is the money raised by issuing equity (shares in the business), and is often seen at the initial and growth stages of a business. There are also **retained profits**, where a portion of profits from sales is saved as a buffer against tough times. And of course, **debt** is money owed to a third party that you have to repay (typically with interest), such as a mortgage, lease agreement or hire purchase agreement.

Money comes in, and money goes out. That's called the *cash conversion cycle*. This is an infinite game as long as you never run out of cash. So, the objective in this infinite game has always got to be that you bring in more cash than you spend.

Let's look at an example of how this might appear in the real world.

## Emma's Coffee Shop

Meet Emma. She's planning to open a small neighbourhood café that provides delicious coffee and cabinet food, as well as a warm and welcoming space for customers to sit and consume their purchases. Emma's goal is also to make a sustainable profit based on a simple financial model. In this book we will be accompanying

Emma on her journey as she launches and operates her new business, exploring with her the key financial components and functions that underpin a business or organisation.

Emma's been saving money for Emma's Coffee Shop for a while. She also has a bank **loan**, and some **investments** from friends and family. This is her *starting capital.* And it's the opening balance of the business.

If a business is funded solely on debt — for example, an overdraft in a cheque account — then the business's opening balance can be negative. This is especially true if the value of the bank loan is larger than any savings or investments. A situation like this is riskier than having a positive total opening balance, but sometimes cannot be avoided.

Emma uses some of this opening balance to buy furniture and a fit-out (**assets**), and to pay for a coffee machine and other supplies like coffee beans, milk, sugar, kitchen ingredients, cleaning products, and so on (**stock**). She uses some of the money to hire and train baristas and other staff (**people**), and to pay for rent and power on the premises (**expenses**). This reduces her cash balances; the cash pot gets low.

When she opens Emma's Coffee Shop, however, Emma starts making **sales**. The money she makes from selling coffee and food goes into that cash pot to top it up. It then goes out again to pay for more **stock** and **staff**, back in again with further **sales**, and so on.

These are the fundamentals of business. Perhaps so far, this is all feeling fairly obvious or familiar to you. But to be able to move forward it's important that we get a solid groundwork of terminology and of the flow of money taking place. Having said that, it's also helpful to recognise that there are many more complexities within these more recognisable terms.

For example, there are multiple types of costs. *Fixed costs* cover those that you expect to be the same month-by-month, like rent or staff salaries. *Variable costs* will vary depending on the output, such as how many coffee beans are used depending on how many coffees are sold. There are also *one-time costs*, which will have benefits over many years. For Emma this might be a new coffee machine or a website redesign. Knowing how these relate to the business — and how money flows to them with time — is important for getting an idea of the bigger picture. But let's park that thought for now.

The important thing to recognise is that, while sales revenue and profit are important, having sufficient cash *flow* is much more critical for a business's survival and growth. As the saying goes: Sales is vanity, profit is sanity, and cash is king.

Cash is not a 'nice to have'; it's necessary for any organisation to thrive. It is the lifeblood of your organisation. And if that lifeblood is not moving through an organisation — coming in, going out, driving action — then you come to a stop. An organisation can have impressive sales figures and

Cash is not a 'nice to have'; it's necessary for any organisation to thrive. It is the lifeblood of your organisation.

even paper profits, but without adequate cash reserves or positive cash flow (where the cash coming in exceeds the cash going out), it risks running out of cash and the organisation failing. Even profitable businesses can fail without sufficient cash to meet short-term needs.

Conversely, positive cash flow enables an organisation to meet its financial obligations and be more likely to weather any political, environmental, social, economic or legislative impacts. Having ample cash reserves provides greater autonomy, reducing the need for external borrowing and allowing a business to make key decisions independently. These reserves also act as fuel for future growth and investment, lessening reliance on outside funding. Effective cash management means you can seize opportunities, such as taking advantage of discounts or even acquiring other businesses.

Consistent positive cash flow is also a strong indicator of financial health, pleasing investors and even allowing for dividend payouts.

If you remember nothing else from this chapter, let it be this: cash is the most critical thing in any organisation.

## Different kinds of cash flow

Many businesses make losses for years before turning a profit. Despite having revenues of $1.6 billion in 1999, Amazon only turned a profit in 2003, nine years after being founded and seven years after going public.[2] Uber made its first full-year profit in 2024, 15 years after being founded.[3]

Just like a human body can't function without blood, an organisation can't function without cash (I know I keep hammering on about this, but it is so critical). Just as when you cut yourself you put a plaster over the cut to stop the blood flow, you can manage cash outflows by cutting expenses and putting a stop on wasteful spending.

Although to most people cash is cash, accountants make distinctions about cash based on where it came from or what it is used for. It's helpful to know the difference so that you can understand where your money is coming from and where you need to make strategic moves to improve your cashflow.

**Operating cash flow** refers to the cash that comes and goes from the day-to-day running of the organisation. It's the money you get from customers when they buy your products or services, the money you pay suppliers and employees, and the money you use for other regular expenses like rent and utilities. This type of cash is important to understand because it shows whether your organisation can generate enough cash from its operations to sustain itself.

The next kind is the **investing cash flow**, which is involved in buying and selling long-term assets or investments like equipment or property, and it shows what you are investing in future growth.

The last kind is the **financing cash flow**. This is the cash that moves in and out of the organisation related to financing your organisation, such as interest payments, new loans or repaying loans, shares, and dividends, and it shows how your business is financed and how you are managing your financial resources.

## Cash conversion cycles

As pointed out earlier, if you run out of cash, then it's game over. You can't continue to trade with no money. So the objective is to make sure the cash pot is topped up more quickly than it is emptied.

That's why so many businesses are interested in the cash cycle or the **cash conversion cycle (CCC)**. This measures the time it takes for a company to convert its investments in inventory and other resources into cash flows from sales. The cash conversion cycle reveals how quickly your organisation can turn investments in inventory and other resources back into cash, which in turn directly impacts its ability to pay bills, seize growth opportunities, and avoid cash shortfalls.

The longer the CCC, the more cash you need to keep operations going; a faster cash cycle means you will be generating and growing your cash much more quickly.

As a budget leader, managing the CCC is essential for maintaining healthy business operations and ensuring sufficient liquidity (accessible cash) to meet financial obligations. One way to do that is to decrease or shorten the number of days in your cash conversion cycle, so that cash is moving back through your business sooner and can be put to more work.

While there's no universal "gold standard" number of days, a shorter CCC is generally more desirable, as it means your business recovers cash faster and operates more efficiently; however, what's considered optimal will vary by industry and business model.

Emma's Coffee Shop will have a relatively short cash cycle, because it involves fast-moving goods: beans and food items aren't held long before they sell. If Emma were to branch out into off-site catering, she might have a longer cash cycle, if the goods and services involved are to be invoiced at a later date.

For manufacturers, however, a cycle can be in the order of months or even stretch to a year. Take the example of a friend of mine in the UK who was looking to strike a deal sourcing parts offshore on behalf of a UK car manufacturer. The parts, which would be made in Korea, had to be paid for three months in advance, but the car manufacturer in the UK would only pay for the parts six months after receiving them. While this worked really well for both of the manufacturers, it meant my friend would need sufficient cash flow to cover at least nine months of cash outgoings before he'd see any sales money coming back into his business. And of course that was only for the first month of sales. At the end of the first month, he'd have to place another order and pay up-front for that. As you can imagine, no matter how great the deal, no bank was willing to lend him the money to finance his cash flow

Some organisations, such as supermarkets, are great examples of *negative* CCC businesses because they get paid by their customers *before* they pay their suppliers. They might receive their apples on day one and sell them the same day, but only have to pay their suppliers once every 30 days, giving a 29-day cycle. This is not entirely uncontroversial, and does make it harder for suppliers (especially smaller suppliers) to meet their own cash flow needs, but it suits the supermarkets very well.

Your CCC is going to depend on a range of factors — including your suppliers and customers — and shortening it will keep the cash flowing through your business. But as long as it's flowing, you're on the right track.

Still, all of these potential permutations mean you need to make sure that all of the elements that make up your organisation's specific cash flow picture align and allow unimpeded flow. Knowing where your cash is coming from and when, and where and when it's going, gives you a clear map of your organisation's financial health. You can spot whether your day-to-day operations actually fund themselves, if you're investing wisely in future growth, and how heavily you rely on debt or equity. That way, you can make smarter decisions about where to cut back, where to invest more, and how to structure your financing.

> Many organisations don't generate a profit for a long time, which is an issue because profit is the source of operating cash.

Many organisations don't generate a profit for a long time, which is an issue because profit is the source of operating cash. Where there is no profit, or a delay in realising profit, for the organisation keep running, it needs either cash input from the owner or investors, or sufficient borrowings in the form of loans in order to keep it going until the operating cash flows are sufficient to sustain the business. This is why investors (and I'll include the bank lending officer in that) are so interested in understanding your organisation's cash flow through cash flow forecasts — the plan of when you expect money to come in and when you expect it to go out.

In most commercial transactions, sales are made on **credit terms**. This means that when you sell something, there's a period between invoicing the sale and receiving the cash. The time can vary based on the terms negotiated as part of the sale.

But for the sake of simplicity, let's say that if you made a sale today you'd get the cash from the customer this time next month. This is part of the cash cycle, as described above. So, in your cash flow forecast, you'd have no money coming in this month. But you'd still have expenses to pay, which would be recorded as cash going out. So, when the cash outgoings exceed the cash incomings, you have negative cash flow. Unless you have sufficient money in the bank (or can access it quickly, such as through an overdraft or bank loan), you won't be able to continue to trade, and will be insolvent.

Continuing to trade while insolvent is not only reckless, it's illegal, which could have severe repercussions if you're a director or owner of the business. In Australia, for directors that could be civil penalties (fines up to A$200,000), personal liability for any debts incurred while insolvent, disqualification as a director, and up to 10 years in prison.

But in this case let's assume you have received payment and can carry on trading.

So when we are talking about improving cash flow, we're talking about improving *operating* cash flow. This is because as a budget holder you'll have very little ability to improve financing cash flow and limited ability to improve investing cashflow.

## Improving operating cash flow

There are three areas that can be focused on to improve the cash conversion cycle.

The first is *inventory management*, such as reducing the stock levels you have on hand, simplifying product design so that you need less inventory, and ensuring that stock is turned over regularly. Many businesses run out of money yet have warehouses full of inventory. That's why you see so many retailers run end-of-season sales — to top up their cash supplies in order to pay for the following season's goods (not just to annoy you with ads everywhere!).

The second is to *improve payment terms with suppliers.* By concentrating your sources of supply (i.e. by reducing the actual number of suppliers you deal with), loyalty and economies of scale may mean you will be able to get better payment terms, including longer pay times.

Thirdly, you can *collect money from customers more quickly*, improving your cash flow. This could be achieved by reducing the credit terms you give customers, but, let's be honest, that's not going to go down too well with customers, especially if your competitors offer the same or better credit terms. When this is the case, the only real opportunity you have is to offer discounts to customers for prompt payment. Giving a discount will reduce the amount you have coming in, but the reduced time with the outstanding sales might make the discount worthwhile (or at least make it worth exploring!).

Okay, now that you understand cash, the very basic terms that surround cash, and how it flows in and out of a business, there is just one last thing that it's important to cover before we dig into The 3 Fs — financial reports ...

CHAPTER TWO

# Understanding financial reports

As a budget holder, you're probably come across financial reports many times before. Maybe you're at the point now where you can skim through them without your heart racing, but if you still see one and go pale with dread, that's okay. Many non-financial leaders — even highly expert ones with years of experience — still hold a (mostly figurative) crucifix up to their monthly report.

I don't want to get too bogged in what can quick become a mire of financial reporting detail, as much of what we'll cover in The 3 Fs will help you navigate this adequately. But let's quickly go over the key elements that might show up in a report just so we're all on the same page.

These include:

- the **income statement**, which shows revenues, expenses, profit and loss
- the **balance sheet**, which shows assets, liabilities and equity

- the **cash flow statement**, which breaks down the cash movement across operating, investing and financing activities, and
- the **statement of changes in equity**, which details how the equity balances have evolved.

When you know how to read these documents, you can see if and how the day-to-day operations are (self-)funding, whether you're investing wisely, and how to plan and grow for the future.

Since we're talking a lot about cash, let's focus on that — especially since cash can be deceptive in a financial report.

When you're dealing with home finances, you generally think in terms of cash: you get paid, allocate the money to various expenses, and save what you have left over (in theory, at least!). This is called cash accounting, and it's a perfectly straightforward way of understanding what's going on in the moment.

But a business makes commitments today that have impacts in the future. The impact of these decisions might not be seen until next week or even a few months from now. Emma, for example, pays for her coffee beans monthly: currently she owes $1,000, but she hasn't paid for it yet so it hasn't left her bank account. But while she might have $1,000 sitting in the bank account, because it's owed to someone, her accountants will make adjustments to reflect the $1,000 outstanding debt (liability), and will earmark the $1,000 sitting in the account to pay the coffee bean supplier.

A liability goes the other way, too: where you have been paid for something that you are yet to earn or provide. For example, an executive coach gets paid $12,000 in advance to provide coaching over the next 12 months: while their bank account will show the full $12,000, the financial report will show only $1,000 in earnings (i.e. $12,000/12 months). This is because while the customer might have paid the executive coach the full amount today, 11/12 of that income relates to future periods of work which is yet to be done.

Sounds pretty straightforward, right? Now imagine you're dealing in hundreds of thousands or millions of dollars. Getting a handle on your money means looking way beyond just the number showing in your bank account, because, as I've just shown, it can be pretty deceptive if you treat it as face-value cash. This is why financial reports are often difficult to understand: what you think should have happened based on your experiences frequently isn't reflected in the accounts.

> While a good bank balance feels secure, it's only one piece of a much bigger, more complex financial puzzle.

While a good bank balance feels secure (and what makes a good balance is the subject of a whole other conversation), it's only one piece of a much bigger, more complex financial puzzle. You also need to understand how much you owe and how much you're owed, and (just as importantly) when you expect to pay or be paid.

All of this is why you shouldn't rely on point-in-time information (e.g. how much money is shown in your bank account) to make good decisions.

## Why financial reports feel so overwhelming — and how to overcome the overwhelm

Reports are designed by — and for — accountants. That's why they're usually structured around accounting codes, rules, standards, compliance, and categories that don't map directly to your operations, your team's delivery, or your strategy.

That being said, financial reports can be incredibly helpful to *all* leaders — so long as you have your own appropriate frame to interpret and make sense of them. I'll walk you through a simple way to do this.

When you look at a financial report, ask:

- What does this number actually mean?
  *For example, if it's revenue or income, think "money coming in"; an expense, think "money going out"; a provision, think "an accounting adjustment".*
- What story is the report telling me about inputs and outputs?
  *Look at what changes have occurred, especially around your overall spending or your overall earning.*
- Does this align with what I expected to see?
  *Pay special attention to numbers that have shifted dramatically.*

Another important term to consider is your **variance.** A variance is simply comparing what you thought you would spend (budget) against what you have actually spent (actual).

For expenditure, in simple terms a *negative variance* is classed as "bad" (i.e. you spent more than you budgeted). A *positive variance* is classed as "good". However, neither of these things means anything on its own.

Think back to the story I told earlier about working with a social housing organisation that was investing less than it had planned in construction. As a consequence, the variance was positive. The financial commentary that went with the report was complimentary, as the construction team had spent less than planned. However, compared with what the construction team had planned to do (i.e. how many houses they'd planned to build), they were behind the plan. So the underspend was actually a bad thing. The important thing isn't the numbers — it's the story they're telling you.

When I work with Finance teams to help them become more influential, I teach them to describe variances using three levels of "what":

1. **What?** What happened? (e.g. the construction team spent less than planned)
2. **So What?** What will the impact be? (e.g. unless the construction team steps up activity over the next month, we will be behind target).
3. **Now What?** What do we do now? (e.g. the construction team needs to replan activity to ensure the build targets can be achieved)

If you find or discover a variance in your report, you can do a simple variance analysis to find out more. This is as simple as just asking a few probing questions like the ones above to get some context or reasoning around the variance. Ask what changed in the activity or environment that influenced the result. Was the budget wrong? Was there a timing issue? Did something unexpected happen? Essentially, it's about figuring out whether it's something you should be concerned about or not — and where there might be an opportunity to right any wrongs.

We'll be getting into many more examples of how to formulate questions, how to dig out the information that matters, and much more in the coming chapters. For now, just remember that a financial report is basically a reflection of your basic financial numbers — and that making sense of them can be as simple as thinking big picture, being thoughtful, and asking the right questions.

## It's time to move from understanding to application

You should now have a pretty clear overview of the essentials. The terminology that often comes up in conversations with the Finance team, the principles of what cash actually means and how it moves, and the primary elements of a financial report.

Next, we're going to put these basics into context and practise. To get there, we're going to lean on a simple framework that I'll take you through for the rest of this book.

## The 3 Fs: our path forward

In my experience, the simpler the better. Understanding numbers and being able to engage with how they work in your business doesn't require an accounting degree. Or even a maths lesson. It's all about grasping *what the numbers mean.* No complicated maths! I promise. Just a simple approach to help you engage in a more effective way with financial matters.

It looks like this:

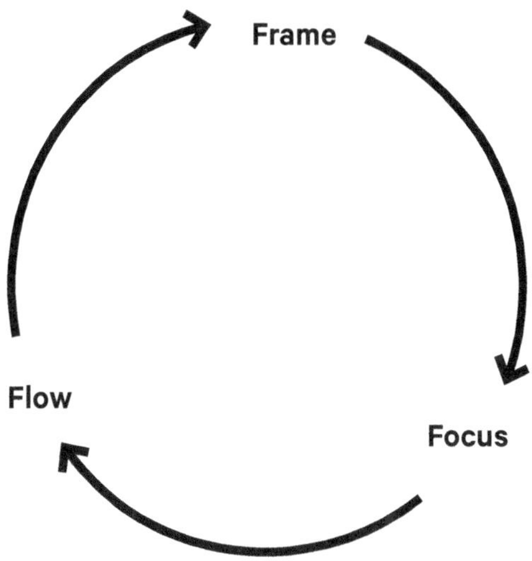


When The 3 Fs come together — Frame, Focus and Flow — they help board members, executives, leaders, and anyone else without a background in finance become much more confident in their approach. It's less about "getting" the numbers and maths, and more about being able to communicate and collaborate effectively with the people who do. By the end of this book, you'll be sitting comfortably right in the middle of those circles.

The first element is **Frame** — that is, how you view your organisation.

Think of your car's dashboard. It'll tell you all the basic information you need to know while driving: whether you have enough fuel (or how much charge you have left), how fast you're going, whether you should have topped up with oil, how late you are to a meeting … You don't need to know *how* the various gauges on your dashboard work in order to understand the basic information they are giving — say, your speed on the speedometer — and then use that basic information to drive to the conditions.

Framing is about understanding how the processes in your business all interconnect and disconnect...

When it comes to finances, there are similarly a few key models and systems which can give you your own business dashboard. Likewise, if you understand how to read them, you can get the immediate and important information you need without actually having to fully comprehend the daunting machinations that produce the numbers.

Framing is about understanding how the processes in your business all interconnect and disconnect, allowing you to examine smaller elements or zoom out to view the bigger picture. When you start to understand all of the component pieces, you can begin designing your own models, too. For example, as a manager you could create a model for your area of responsibility. If you're a business unit director you could develop a model that connects all of the individual areas into one overarching representation of what's going on. (Don't worry: if that feels overwhelming right now, it won't by the time we get there!)

Once you have a model, you can use it to ask your Finance team questions, so you better understand what happens when decisions get made, and how your finances flow through the business.

One of the biggest challenges for people reviewing a finance report is that it consists of seemingly abstract elements, which, unless you have a solid understanding of accounting, aren't easy to piece together. Framing provides a structured and visual way to interpret financial data. While it's possible to create a model for almost any situation, having a simple, approach you can repeat any time you need to, makes it easier to adapt when you move into new roles or take on different teams. A good model allows you to isolate key financial drivers and ensures that decision-making is based on clarity, not guesswork.

Once you have a model, the next step is **Focus** — identifying which areas are the most critical. Too often, leaders learn about finance through experience and anecdote, which leads to reinforcing common misunderstandings or focusing on the wrong thing.

For instance, when reviewing a financial report, a leader might notice a cost item with a negative variance — where actual costs exceed the budget — and instinctively assume it's a problem.

In finance reports, negative variances are often shown in parentheses, leading many to believe that anything in parentheses is bad. But context is everything. Just because an expense is higher than budgeted doesn't necessarily mean it's represents a negative outcome. Take travel costs, for example. If a company incurs unexpected travel expenses that weren't in the budget, that variance might seem like an issue. However, if that travel resulted in securing an unexpected million-dollar contract, the overspend is irrelevant.

Unfortunately, many leaders have been conditioned to focus on variances as negative indicators rather than asking whether an overspend was productive. This kind of tunnel vision and accompanying assumptions can lead to wasted time. For example, a budget holder might question an unexpected but fairly innocuous expense, prompting the Finance team to investigate it and report back, only to discover that the expense was completely justified. Instead of spending time chasing down a fairly inconsequential line item, the team could have been spent that time uncovering more significant financial insights.

For non-finance leaders, the key is not to understand every aspect of the budget but to focus on the most critical elements. Without focus, it's easy to get lost in the noise and miss what truly impacts performance. Again, it is a matter of knowing which signals on the dashboard are significant and need your attention, and then responding to them appropriately, rather than being distracted by every little element and wasting everyone's time by asking for an expert explanation of each of them.

The final phase is about bringing everything together: **flow**. The goal here is to help you flow into action as you bring your financial framing and focus into how you actually engage with financial conversations and make strategic decisions for your business.

In large part, flow depends on better, stronger collaboration with your Finance team — so we'll have a thorough look at how to ask more strategic questions to drive better conversations and clearer outcomes.

One of the advantages of not being a finance expert is that you have fresh eyes and don't suffer from the "curse of expertise". This term refers to the tendency of experts to forget what it is like to be a beginner. Finance teams often struggle to explain concepts in simple terms because they assume a baseline level of knowledge that many non-financial leaders don't have. By maintaining a fresh perspective and asking questions that challenge assumptions, you can cut through jargon and get to the heart of financial issues.

One of the advantages of not being a finance expert is that you have fresh eyes and don't suffer from the "curse of expertise".

Simply put: understanding finance isn't about memorising accounting rules. It's about using models to simplify complexity, focusing on what truly matters, and asking the right questions to unlock insights. When leaders embrace these three elements, finance becomes less intimidating and far more valuable.

By integrating The 3 Fs into your approach, you'll move from passive recipient to active participant in financial discussions, driving better decisions and better outcomes for your organisation. We'll look at how you can conceptualise money as it runs through your business, how to determine which elements or metrics to pay attention to as money and finance relates to your role and business priorities, and how to then use these core pieces of understanding to have better, more thoughtful conversations with your finance team.

If you find yourself forgetting what a certain term means, or losing track of how it all fits together, just return to this chapter and track down the appropriate section for a quick refresher. Yes, finance really can be simple — but that doesn't mean you should expect yourself to learn all the terminology or remember the concepts after just reading this once.

So, with that in mind and this ready-reckoner chapter backing you up, let's get into the fun stuff! We'll start back with our first F — Frame — and explore how your business and your finances fit together. Let's do this, my friend.

# PART TWO

# FRAME

*Without a frame, finance is just noise. With a frame, it's insight.*

CHAPTER THREE

# Why Framing Matters

Now that you understand the basics of financial terms and how the pieces fit together, let's start to make sense of them.

Ever feel like you open a report and just see a bunch of numbers flying around? Like all you can do is freeze and just admire the whooshing sound as they fly over your head?

In my experience, the primary reason leaders feel like they struggle to engage with finance is because it's too abstract and they have no frame of reference in which to place it and see how it relates to their particular area of practice. They're being asked to look at a spreadsheet or analyse a report, all without actually understanding the bigger picture context of what they're working with.

So, let's build a Frame, our first "F" of the book.

## A Frame is your architectural blueprint

Imagine walking onto an active building site. At first, it might feel like total chaos; materials everywhere, loud noises, workers

> In my experience, the primary reason leaders feel like they struggle to engage with finance is because it's too abstract...

engaged in various tasks in every corner. To someone who doesn't know anything about building, it's going to be a little intimidating. More than that, it's almost impossible to gauge whether the work is being done to a high standard and being completed efficiently.

Now imagine that before you walk into that busy worksite, you're given a copy of the building's architectural blueprint and the project plan. Maybe the project manager takes a moment to explain how all of the various pieces and tasks and side-projects will come together.

With this little bit of context, you might start to see the correlation between that loud dropsaw at work over there and the kitchen cabinetry plans. The more comfortable you get with reading and understanding the blueprint and the project plan, the more the work around you starts to make sense. Once you get really comfortable with it all, you might start to pick up on opportunities for improvement. You might ask smarter questions, or even pose some strategic challenges, such as why things are done in a particular order.

You don't have to *be* a builder to "get" what's going on. You don't have to learn the nuts and bolts (or woodscrews) to understand the project as a whole. And the same is true for finances. Without needing to be a finance expert, you can begin to understand how things connect — and, more importantly, how your role impacts and is impacted by finances.

A good Frame is your architectural blueprint. It's being able to connect what's happening financially in your organisation with actual action and impact. It essentially allows you to:

- visualise how money flows through your organisation
- see how activity connects to finances
- filter out what matters from what doesn't
- feel confident in your own interpretation of what's happening financially
- ask better questions and spark better conversations with your Finance team.

The way we get there is by tapping into a model I've designed specifically for non-financial leaders — The Performance Conversation Model. Rather than relying on a mountain of overwhelming spreadsheets to track information, this model works more like a flowchart. The idea is to give you a simple, easy-to-leverage tool that helps you zoom out, conceptualise what's happening, and have some context before you start digging into the actual financial numbers.

And here's the best part: you *already* have all the knowledge and tools you need to take on Framing. The beauty of this section of The 3 Fs model it's not about maths — it's about making connections and visualising relationships. And that kind of thinking is what you (with that enviable expert mind of yours!) are already good at. I won't ask you to actually do any calculations here. Instead, you can just lean on a pen and a stack of Post-its, scribble in your notebook or use tablet to work your way through this model.

But before we get to discussing this model, though, we need to have a general understanding of what models are, how we can use them, and what they're good for.

## How framing depends on models

I realise that up until now I've been throwing this term out there — "model" — without showing exactly what it means. So let's consider what we're creating.

Again, an example from childhood offers a useful starting point. When I was a kid I liked building model aeroplanes. I'd spend hours pressing out all of the little parts from the plastic sheets and gluing them all together (or, more often that not, sticking my finger to the part). After painstakingly putting every piece together, I'd end up with something that looked like the real thing. A model aeroplane is essentially a representation of a real aeroplane but using different materials and at a much smaller scale. Nevertheless, when you put together a model aeroplane you learn about each part, what purpose it serves, and how it should work "in the real world".

Business models work in a similar way — but they go a little deeper. They are used to succinctly and strategically outline how your business works, and their "parts" include things like "product for sale" and "target market" and "production processes".

The models we're going to use in this context are the model aeroplanes of your organisation. They're a summarised representation of how each piece of your business fits together — and specifically, how the money flows through it.

It's important to note that there are countless "off-the-shelf" models out there that you can use to try to do this in different ways. There's a model for every level of complexity, type of business, role or perspective, and purpose. However, not all models are helpful. Some are so vague that they're meaningless; others are so complicated that they require a PhD and a pack of paracetamol just to interpret them. So how do you know when a model is actually useful?

You look for the **Goldilocks Zone.**

A good model lives in the sweet spot: not too hot, not too cold. It's not built purely on gut feel and guesswork (too cold), but nor is it a 17-page flow chart with connector tabs pointing to sub-models or process descriptions (too hot). Instead, it's *just structured enough* to explain what's really going on.

It's a bit like when you have a cup of coffee with your friend and draw boxes on a napkin to explain what it is your team or organisation does. (Or, wait, is it just me who does this?)

A well-designed model simplifies complexity. It filters the noise and presents the key variables that affect performance. It helps you see the relationships between activity and outcomes. And, crucially, it gives you a way to talk about money and performance without needing to be an accountant.

So before we dive into The Performance Conversation Model, let's look at a couple of well-established examples of what a basic model can do for you, each representing one of the two fields of vision you need to be clear on: business (external) and organisation (internal).

### 1. *Business models (external focus)*

Business models help you understand how your organisation creates, delivers and captures value. They provide a visual bird's-eye view of what you offer, to whom, and how you generate revenue. They're really helpful when you're developing new or existing modes of delivery. But while a business model sweeps wide for information, it doesn't delve into too much detail about the internal organisational dynamics, such as your operations and how money flows through your business (we'll get to that side of things in a moment).

> Business models help you understand how your organisation creates, delivers and captures value.

A popular business model tool is Alexander Osterwalder's Business Model Canvas, a simple, nine-box framework that breaks your business down into nine interconnected components. I have chosen this particular model over the myriad business model tools available because it's both straightforward and comprehensive. According to Osterwalder, these are the building blocks of your business:

- **Customer segments:** Who are you serving?
- **Value propositions:** What problem are you solving for them?
- **Channels:** How do you deliver value?
- **Customer relationships:** How do you engage your customers?
- **Revenue streams:** How do you make money?
- **Key resources:** What assets do you need?
- **Key activities:** What must you do to deliver value?
- **Key partnerships:** Who helps you do it?
- **Cost structure:** What does it cost to deliver?

If you consider all of these elements, you'll end up with a rough sketch of what your business does, how and where it makes money, and what's most important in terms of staying viable and sustainable as a business. It's a great tool for budget holders or start-ups to ask questions about financial aspects such as cost structure and revenue streams. It can help you explore how changes in these building blocks — or *value chains* — might improve financial performance and align with your overall organisational strategy.

The Business Model Canvas is a fantastic resource during start-up phases, strategic planning sessions, innovation brainstorming workshops, or anytime when your leadership team is working on alignment strategies.

### 2. *Organisational models (internal focus)*

While business models help you look outward, organisational models are designed to help you look inward. They diagnose how your team or organisation functions, and, more importantly, where it might be misaligned.

One of the most powerful tools for this, which has been around for decades, is the McKinsey 7S Framework. This model breaks your organisation down into seven key elements (to which I have conveniently added some finance-related questions — you had to know I wouldn't go too long without some finance pulled in):

1. **Strategy: What is your plan?**
   *Are you investing in the areas that matter most? Are your cost reductions aligned with long-term value, or are they reactive to a current issue?*
2. **Structure: How is your team organised?**
   *Is your team clear on what they own and what they don't? Do reporting lines make sense?*
3. **Systems: What systems and processes support the work?**
   *Is it clear what you are supposed to do when you see the financial or a forecasting report?*
4. **Shared values: What beliefs bind the culture together?**
   *What do the organisation's financial decisions say about what is valued?*
5. **Style: How do leaders lead?**
   *Are leaders transparent and collaborative when they have financial conversations?*

6. **Staff: Who's on the team?**
   *Is everyone on the same page? Does everyone understand how the model connects them all together?*
7. **Skills: What capabilities exist?**
   *Do your people have the skills and mindset to make good decisions about money and investments?*

The 7S model is especially helpful when things aren't working and you can't quite put your finger on why, because it encourages you to look at the soft and hard elements of the organisation alongside each other.

It's a great tool to help budget holders understand how internal alignment and organisational effectiveness affect organisational performance. It can guide questions about whether your resources are aligned with the organisation's strategic goals, and is especially helpful during team change initiatives, restructuring, or when performance is lagging and you suspect that internal friction might be to blame. It's not so great for structurally representing the key processes of your organisation.

These two kinds of models should give you a general idea of what kind of thinking is required for Frame. Note how neither of them asks you to do any sort of mathematical equation; instead they focus on getting you to consider how, where and why different parts of your business exist. However, while both of them are certainly helpful tools that I'd encourage you to try out, also be aware that they do have some limitations. Namely, they stop at reflection instead of moving you towards opportunity-seeking.

The other drawback is that they tend to assume either that you're a start-up with traditional products to sell (which is the kind of business that Osterwalder's book focuses on), or that you're a large corporation (which the McKinsey 7S is best suited for). This means that these popular models aren't as applicable for non-traditional businesses or internal departmental function.

Luckily for you, I have created a model to bridge this gap and to suit a much larger range of business areas and business types. It has been designed specifically for people like you — non-financial leaders who want to better understand finance so that they can make stronger decisions for their business. So, if you're ready to be introduced to The Performance Conversation Model, and you want to know how to leverage it to better understand and conceptualise finances — read on.

CHAPTER FOUR

# Using the Financial Framing Model

The Financial Framing Model is a practical tool that links strategy, structure and finance into a single view, which I have developed through years of working with non-financial leaders. The model bridges the gap between high-level strategy and the day-to-day realities of budgets, operations and team activity into an organised frame for leaders. This enables it to help you to:

- visualise how six crucial business and money elements intersect and overlap in your business
- align your strategy and vision across your business area, and
- identify the most important elements of your operations and your value.

It looks like this:

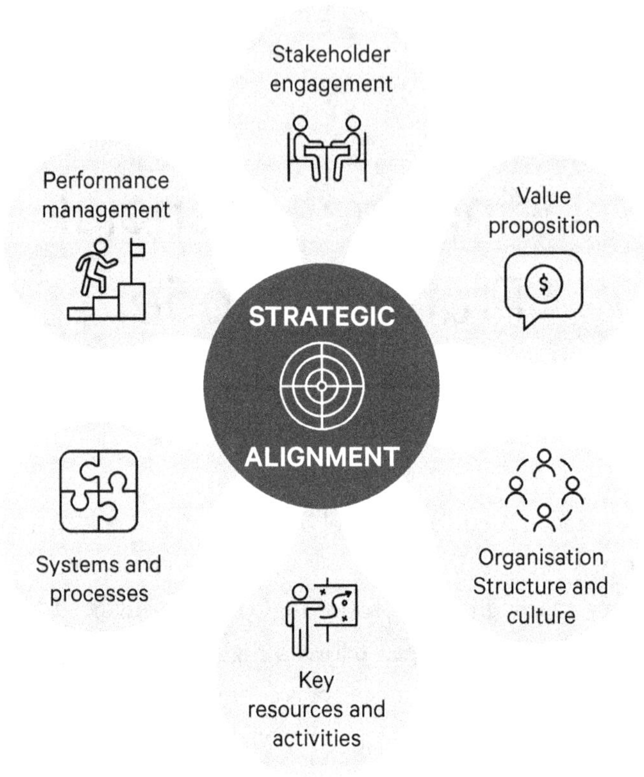


It holds your **Strategic alignment** right at the centre — with six key areas all feeding into it:

1. **Value proposition**
2. **Organisation Structure and culture**
3. **Key resources and activities**
4. **Systems and processes**
5. **Performance management**
6. **Stakeholder engagement.**

Let's go through these elements and apply them to Emma's Coffee Shop as our business sample.

## Applying the model to a business

### *Strategic alignment*

The model starts in the centre and focuses on the organisation's **strategic alignment**, that is: What are we trying to achieve?

Here, in answering this question in relation to your own business you will want to think about your overarching vision and also the impact of your business. Essentially, why do you exist and how will you make it sustainable?

> For Emma, we could imagine that her strategy is built on a deep awareness of both her local community and her knowledge of making and serving coffee. The strategy might be around providing the best coffee in town combined with an awesome ambiance that customers like to be in. She knows that this will set her apart from other coffee shops in her area, and will help her develop a strong, consistent customer base.

### *Value proposition*

From there, we can move on to the **value proposition:** Who are we creating value for, and what are we promising them? For example, Emma would want to consider whether she is intending to primarily serve office workers who might want to grab a coffee and go. Or perhaps, if the location of her shop is more residential, her clientele will be geared more to busy mums catching up with each other, and who need space to park their buggies and comfy seats to sit in and chat while their babies are sleeping. It's important to get as clear about this as possible. This entails you examining what you offer your customers. For internal functions where you provide services to the rest of the organisation, you're looking to define why your function exists and what people would notice if your team didn't show up to work tomorrow.

> Emma's value proposition might be something like: "I serve the tastiest coffee in a setting that feels just as welcoming and cosy as being at home. That way, coffee lovers come to me to enjoy the entire experience — enjoying the space, connecting with others." See how this doesn't just show what she offers, but also highlights what the value of that offer is to the customer?

> Consider how your own business delivers value, and who is the recipient of that value.

Consider how your own business delivers value, and who is the recipient of that value. Then ask yourself how impactful that value is: What would your customers be missing if you stopped existing?

### *Structure and culture*

Next is the organisational **structure and culture.** This allows us to examine three things. First, does your organisational structure support your ability to deliver on the strategy, and does it reflect your priorities? Second, how flexible is it to change if priorities change? And third, how does your culture meet the needs of the business and build high performance?

> Emma's structure is fairly straightforward: it's a classic hospitality operation with baristas, front-counter attendants, and a couple of bakers who come in early. More important is the culture that Emma creates. She knows that to deliver on her promise of a positive, awesome atmosphere it's important to have friendly, relaxed staff. Even when the shop gets really busy, the working structure needs to support faster delivery without stressing her people out and risking transmitting those feelings of stress to the customers.

### *Key resources and activities*

Then, we look at the business's **key resources and activities**, which asks what assets and actions — like people, technology, infrastructure — are essential for delivering value and achieving strategic goals.

> If we think about Emma's case study, we might think of elements such as staffing, point-of-sale machines, a card machine, menu boards, café equipment, waste and recycling bins, etc. Beyond just the basics, we can also think about what might set Emma apart from others. For example, what if she has a far larger or fancier coffee machine than the local café standard? Perhaps this could allow two baristas to work at once, or set her coffee at a higher standard.

### *Systems and processes*

Now it's time to consider how the business actually delivers. A business's **systems and processes** ensure that its key resources and activities are being used and leveraged. The last thing you want is to be reinventing the wheel with every transaction or conversation. The questions to ask are: Do you have clear workflows? Do you leverage technology well? Do you have robust reporting?

Effective systems and processes are crucial for translating strategic goals into tangible financial outcomes and maintaining operational consistency.

> Emma's processes would focus around making coffee and attending to customers in a friendly but quick way. There might be elements here that she's not up to par with: for example, if her staff are taking orders down with a pen and paper instead of a computer, it might be slowing down the process or leading to wrong orders due to human error.

For this element, push yourself to consider what opportunities are out there that you aren't already leveraging.

### *Performance management*

**Performance management** links individual and team activities to strategic goals and financial outcomes. Only when we have clear expectations and monitoring methods can we work pout whether we are growing our business. Effective performance management helps to identify areas of strength and weakness, highlighting any adjustments that may need to be made to budgets, resource allocation, and operational processes. This is where you'll want to look at what kind of changes could impact your growth and productivity.

> For Emma, it might mean looking at how her staff could work faster together, or how to encourage more food sales and larger order sizes. It might mean adding different menu items, or developing new drink options for customers.

Performance management typically involves putting focus, effort or money into a particular project in the hope that it will drive bigger strategic goals. For example, creating a new product that will be easy to upsell, or training the members of your team in a new skill so that they can support your customers at a higher level.

### *Stakeholder engagement*

Finally, **stakeholder engagement** is all about building relationships with everyone who's interested in the business's success, and ensuring that financial decisions consider the needs and perspectives of all of the groups involved. This leads to improved trust, reduced risks, and potentially enhanced financial outcomes.

> Emma's stakeholders are probably limited — perhaps just her and maybe a business partner or an early investor. Maybe it also includes a landlord or even the bank who lent her money at the start of her business. Other invested groups, such a community poetry slam group who use her café once a week for events, might also be considered

> as stakeholders because they have a vested interest in keeping the business running and thriving.
>
> For Emma, stakeholder engagement would probably focus primarily on making sure that she is continuing to benefit from the business, or potentially paying back the initial business loan to her.

For larger, more complex businesses, there could be dozens of stakeholders with varying priorities and interests for the company. For government departments this could be the responsible minister or other government agencies.

Once you've outlined these individual elements for your own situation, it's important to step back and look at them all together. How does each element tie back to your strategic goals? Where are you lacking clarity? Does anything seem unaligned or inconsistent across all of these component areas of your business?

You'll probably run into some other questions as you go through this process — and that's a good thing! The goal of applying this model is to figure out whether anything feels disconnected. To identify any gaps. And, of course, to get clear at the highest level what it is your business actually does and how it all fits together.

## Adding a financial lens

Once you understand the Financial Framing Model, you start to see something really amazing unfold. A direct link starts to appear between abstract, theoretical concepts and concrete realities and stories. Finance is the bridge between these two halves. Real-world impact and effort translates into money, which translates into business impact and flexibility. Essentially, finance is just a realisation of the decisions made by leaders and the consequent actions taken.

I often describe finance like Newton's Third Law of Motion: For every action, there is an equal and opposite reaction. Whenever one object exerts a force on another, the second object exerts an equal force in the opposite direction. When you push on something, it pushes back. And that usually means something starts moving, too.

I often describe finance like Newton's Third Law of Motion: For every action, there is an equal and opposite reaction.

Which is exactly what happens to an organisation's finances when decisions are made.

> *Choose to hire someone → your cash reduces as you pay them, but your output (at least in theory) increases.*
>
> *Don't hire someone → the cash and your output stay the same.*

So when making a decision, it is important to consider what the likely opposite impacts will be of that decision. If you invest in automating a process, what does that do to the workforce? If you update the logo, what does that mean for removing the old logo and rolling out the new one?

So far we have talked a lot about models in terms of the general business, but now it is time to overlay financial models so we can read and interpret financial reports more meaningfully.

A simplified financial model would typically focus on the following:

Income – Costs = Profit (i.e. Surplus)

But that doesn't give you much in the way of actionable insights. That's where the Financial Framing Model comes in. Once you've gone through the steps above and built a really clear understanding of how the key six elements of your business overlap, you're in a great space to start thinking and conversing at the strategic level. From there, you can start adding a financial lens to that conversation.

Essentially, you can add a monetary lens around these five financial elements:

1. **Income:** the source of your cash
2. **Customers/stakeholders:** your value proposition and stakeholder needs/engagement
3. **Resources:** what is needed to deliver the value (e.g. people, raw materials, plant and equipment, buildings, etc.)
4. **Suppliers:** the external systems and processes that ensure the value is delivered, and
5. **Costs:** the expenses of doing business (e.g. council rates, taxes, overheads).

In effect, it takes the income and expenditure account and groups it to areas you can influence, rather than combining controllable and uncontrollable items in a longer list.

The formula looks like this:

Income – (Costs of servicing stakeholders +
Costs of resources + Amounts paid to suppliers +
Costs of doing business) = Profit (i.e. Surplus)

What you have now is not just an overview of what money exists, but also how it directly relates to the operations and strategy of your business. This will help you look more creatively and strategically at the financial evidence in front of you regarding invoices, stakeholders, resources, costs and suppliers.

When your model is clear, your numbers start to make sense. And when your numbers make sense, they become an asset to your leadership and your decision-making.

I designed this model as a kind of catch-all for financial framing. It is broad enough that it keeps your bigger-picture business goals at top of mind, but specific enough that it will get you considering how different inputs (like expenses) and outputs (like sales) affect and are affected by those bigger-picture goals.

### *Quick explainer*

If you're confused as to why I call expenses *inputs* (when the money goes *out* of the business) and sales *outputs* (even though that money comes *into* the business), you're not alone! Here's a quick breakdown:

Think of it like baking a cake. The ingredients are inputs, and the cake that comes out of the oven is the output.

Therefore — once more calling on our friend Emma to provide the example scenario — it follows that the business's expenses are the inputs into coffee-making process (e.g. coffee beans, milk, sugar, barista's time) and the output is the sale of the coffee.

Remember that you don't have to calculate everything yourself — you don't need to *be* the builder! That's why you have a Finance team, after all. The purpose of this model is to frame your understanding of how your business fits together, how things flow, and what important things you need to know about the business's finances to perform your role and advance the business's strategic development.

So once you've got these models to frame up how you see your finances, how do you make sure that these insights help you lead and influence your organisation more effectively and strategically? It's time to lean into purpose.

CHAPTER FIVE

# The Power of Purpose

In his 2009 book *Start with Why,* Simon Sinek talks about the importance of knowing and living your business's "Why". He contends that while most organisations and leaders know what their organisation *does*, and *how* it operates to produce the intended outcomes, they tend to get a little lost when it comes to identifying the deeper purpose and reason for all that effort — their *why*.

When we think about great leadership in general, we invariably identify clear intentionality and aligned purpose as being very important. Given this ground is already so well trodden, through books and speeches and strategic planning meetings, I won't dive in deep here. Instead, I want you to consider how understanding and embracing financial awareness can help you align, promote and focus on purpose more effectively.

This so more than a corporate team-building exercise, for when you are clear about the "why" of your team's existence, you are in a better position to contribute to the organisational priorities, thereby increasing your team's impact.

This clarity also puts you in a better position to collaborate with other areas of the organisation. How the money flows, fuels and enables your team's work offers a crucial insight into whether what you're doing is working. When you have access to a financial report, you're sitting on a gold mine of information — not just regarding money itself, but also about where opportunities exist.

For example, think about the decision-making process around budgets. You want to be able to prioritise spending and investment in areas that add the most value to your organisation and your organisation's purpose. To make those calls strategically, you need to understand things on many different levels — how the money sits currently, what is driving meaningful results, and where other investments are being wasted.

Keep the deeper questions close on hand:

- Why does your team exist?
- What would happen if no one in your team turned up tomorrow?
- What impact would that have on your wider organisation?

These questions are key because the true power of framing depends on you understanding the purpose and the "why" behind everything you do, everyone you work with, and every system you leverage.

If you're sitting here and thinking "Damn, I think I might be way behind on this stuff", then let me reassure you that this reaction is very common. I work with clients all the time who find themselves in need of a little clarity when it comes to their "why".

I'm reminded of a time when I asked the chief operating officer of a large government agency why their functions existed. Instead of getting to the heart of it, they proceeded to tell me what each function *did*. It took several attempts of asking the question over a few meetings before we found the "why". It ended up being something along the lines of: "We help the organisation recruit, develop and retain people in a safe, hazard-free manner and in a way that best leverages technology and resources to allow them to offer the most productive, efficient service to customers." While it might not roll off the tongue too easily, once it was clarified, it was much easier for them to pinpoint where the bottlenecks were and identify what would help them improve their performance. This is because the "why" shifted the focus from the task at hand to the end goal, and with that bigger picture came clarity and an appreciation of there being alternative means and ways of achieving that goal.

The key learning from this is simple: many leaders — even those very high up in organisations — struggle to take a step back from the operations side to get the space and perspective to recognise the reasoning and ultimate purpose behind them.

If this is you, then my advice is to take some time to consider the questions above. And, most importantly, get as clear as you possibly can about your answers to Simon Sinek's questions: What is all the effort going towards? What is the big picture purpose of your organisation or team?

This foundational understanding is part of building a strong Frame, and to nailing this first phase of becoming more financially confident. It's also going to be absolutely crucial when we get to the next F in our framework (Focus), so if you haven't nailed it yet, take a moment, grab a pen and paper, and work through this now!

## Visualising financial realities

Once you have a solid Frame of your team's purpose, it's time to start making connections between what your money is doing and how it's either supporting or hindering that purpose. One of the best ways to work out whether goals are being met is to look at:

- **key drivers** — the factors that influence performance, and
- **trade-offs** — the tensions or decisions that come up regularly.

To see this in practice, let's return to Emma's Coffee Shop.

> The purpose of Emma's Coffee Shop is to provide delicious coffee, and a warm and welcoming space for customers, while at the same time making enough money to pay the bills and reward herself for all the effort she's putting in. To work out whether these goals are being met, a good places to start is looking at two other elements: key drivers and trade-offs. For Emma, it might look like this:
>
> - **Key drivers:** Customer volume, average spend per customer, opening hours

- **Trade-offs:** Hiring more baristas versus extending opening hours, premium beans versus lower coffee prices.

Already we can see how some numbers, ratios and calculations could help Emma make better, conscious, more strategic decisions. We'll get much more into detail about how to leverage better decision-making from models in the next section, Focus, but before we get there let's look at what other tools Emma could lean on to design and read a financial report for her business.

## Financial ratios: the building blocks

Ratios are a way to distil complex financial information into simple indicators. Think of it as like checking your finances' blood pressure or temperature. While it's not a full-body check-up or a CT scan, it should give you a quick snapshot of your immediate health or condition. But, as with most health metrics, a one-off measurement like this gives you insight only into how healthy you are at that point in time. Your heart rate at any one moment doesn't tell you much; a change in your heart rate or your average heart rate over the course of several months, meanwhile, tells you a lot. The same is true for financial ratios: viewed singly they give you a snapshot of a point in time, but it is only when a number of them are compared over time that

Ratios are a way to distil complex financial information into simple indicators.

they tell a story from which meaningful trends may emerge and conclusions be drawn.

Ratios help you zoom in on specific aspects of performance — like liquidity, profitability or efficiency — and can be used to track how things are going over time. In some cases, you'll use a ratio on its own. But more often ratios are also used within larger or more complex models. They're super helpful building blocks, and a great place to start when it comes to building your financial Frame.

There are heaps of ratios out there, but there are three that come up all the time. These are the ones I'd encourage you to commit to memory right now. They are:

- **profit margin**
- **quick ratio (liquidity)**
- **scenario analysis (sensitivity).**

Given their significance and usefulness, let's look at each of them in a little more detail.

### *Profit margin*

This is the percentage of money the business keeps as profit from sales after expenses have been deducted and paid.

> For example, if you sell something for $100 and it costs you $80 to make and sell it, you will have $20 left over — this is your profit.

> This means your profit margin will be 20% (Profit ÷ Sales) x100.

A higher or rising profit margin means that a business is keeping more money from its sales, which allows it to then spend more resources on other things that can grow the business, such as marketing, strategy, product development, or research.

### *Quick ratio (liquidity)*

Also known as the "acid test", this ratio shows how easily a business can pay its short-term debts using its most liquid assets (i.e. those that can be sold quickly for cash). If you were doing a quick ratio for your personal finances, it would be as simple as this:

> You want to buy some sweets. Do you have cash in your pocket for them right now, or money in your cheque account? Or, worryingly, will you have to put it on your credit card and wait until payday to actually pay the debt?

A quick ratio of 1:1 or higher generally means you're in a stable position.

To calculate it, follow this formula:

(Current assets – Stock) ÷ Current liabilities

### *Scenario analysis (sensitivity)*

While this one isn't exactly a ratio, I'm throwing it in here anyway because a scenario analysis, like a ratio, gives you a quick look at a big question. Essentially, a scenario analysis helps you estimate potential changes in the future without going into a detailed prediction of the exact outcomes. It's like a quick, back-of-the-envelope way to answer a question like: What would happen if our sales drop by 10% next year?

Finance teams use this tool for stress testing (an analysis to see how something would perform hypothetically in a crisis), but it's just as helpful at a team level. They're especially useful during meaningful or strategic conversations, so you don't have to get too bogged down with making the most accurate, data-backed predictions.

Again, remember that you don't have to be able to do these calculations yourself to find them helpful. Just understanding what they mean — and then leaning on your Finance team to draw up the actual numbers — is a huge step towards building a solid financial Frame.

Now we're at the point where we have gone through all the pieces: what a model is, how to use it to contextualise your business, the importance of knowing your purpose, and the basic building blocks of financial ratios and terms. So let's put it all together and look at how you can start to construct your own model and begin to build a Frame for your own business's financial reality.

## Tying together models and reports

Let's recap. A good model doesn't need to be complex, clever or even particularly elegant. It just needs to be useful. If you want to take your own interpretation and understanding of your financial report further, this is where you could create your own model, tailored to your role and your business. Essentially, a customised approach to combining your foundational understanding of what's important (i.e. your wider purpose and goals) with the information you already receive (e.g. your monthly financial report).

> A good model doesn't need to be complex, clever or even particularly elegant. It just needs to be useful.

Here are a few core principles to follow when designing a model of your own:

- **Start with simplicity:** If it's too complex to explain to your team in under five minutes, it's too complex.
- **Clarify inputs and outputs:** What drives what? What goes in, and what comes out?
- **Reflect real-world decisions:** Build a model that mirrors the decisions you make, not abstract financial categories.
- **Use it to guide conversations:** A good model helps you talk more clearly and confidently about performance.

The goal is to create something that serves two purposes:

- it helps you better understand the numbers and what they mean, and
- it helps you connect those insights to actual business impacts.

Let's finish this section by actually trying it out.

### *Mocking up a model*

Sketch out a simple model of your own team or budget area. You can do this on a whiteboard, in a notebook, or even on a paper napkin.

Here's what to include:

- **Revenue streams:** Where does the money come from?
- **Cost structure:** What are the major categories of spend?
- **Fixed versus variable versus one-time costs:** What costs change with activity?
- **Key drivers:** What factors influence performance?
- **Trade-offs:** What tensions or decisions come up regularly?

If we sketch these elements out for Emma's business, it will look a little like this (see opposite):

Now, correlate these elements to the numbers you're seeing on your report. Start linking up different revenue sources with the sales you see on the spreadsheet or report. Then look at which numbers could give you insight about your key drivers. For Emma, this might be looking at average customer spend or which hours of the day have turned the most sales. The goal is to link up and answer this question:

What does success look like *financially* —
and what does it feel like *operationally*?

Sketch it, reflect on it, and test it out with your team. The best way to see whether a model works for you is to just give it a go. See

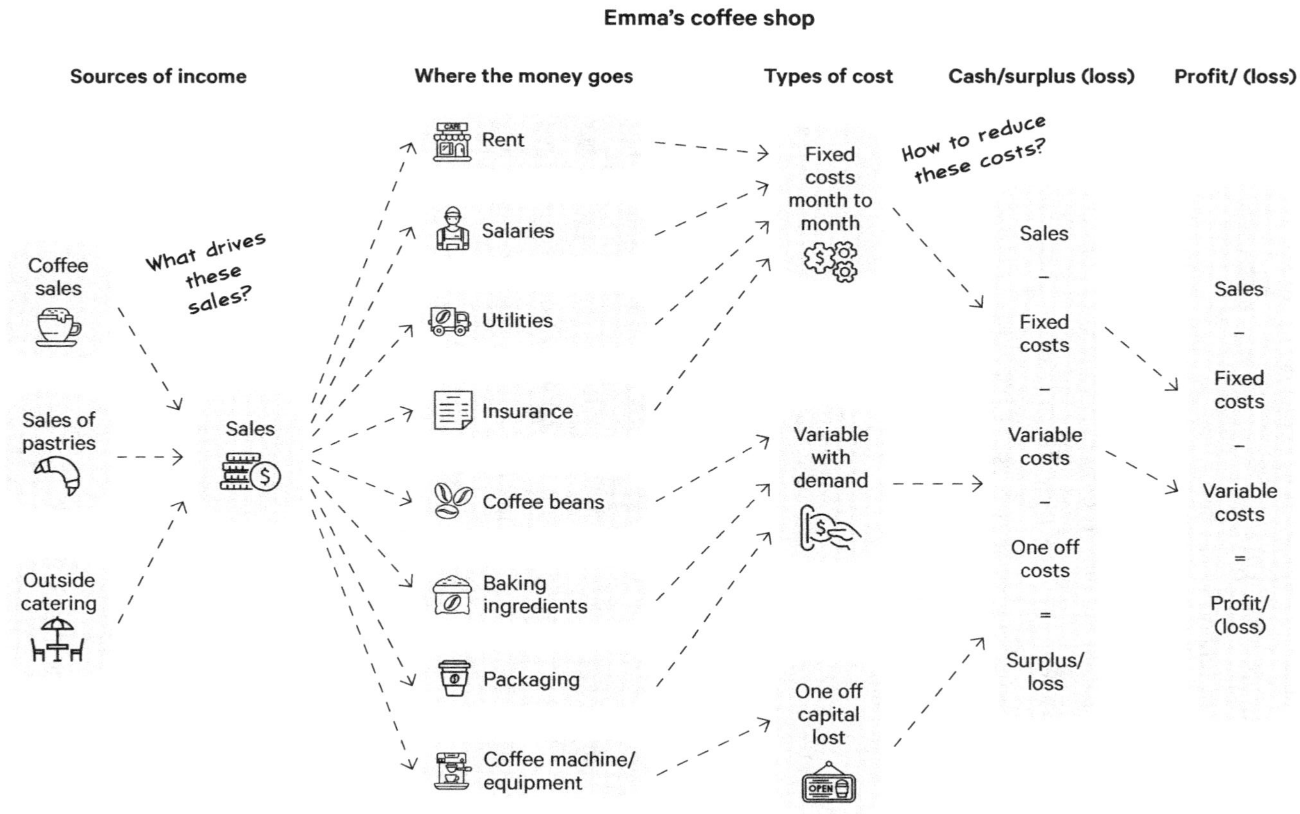
Emma's coffee shop
Sources of income
Where the money goes
Types of cost
Cash/surplus (loss)
Profit/ (loss)
Coffee sales
Sales of pastries
Outside catering
What drives these sales?
Sales
Rent
Salaries
Utilities
Insurance
Coffee beans
Baking ingredients
Packaging
Coffee machine/ equipment
Fixed costs month to month
Variable with demand
One off capital lost
OPEN
How to reduce these costs?
Sales
–
Fixed costs
–
Variable costs
–
One off costs
=
Surplus/ loss
Sales
–
Fixed costs
–
Variable costs
=
Profit/ (loss)

what it helps you find, if it connects any dots, or whether it leads to any interesting (or, at the very least, clarifying!) conversations with others on your team.

If you don't know where to start, go back to the existing, established models I showed you before: the Business Model Canvas and the McKinsey 7S Framework. Then ask yourself what gaps or other questions you have that weren't answered from those insights. From there, start to consider how to get the kind of answers you're looking for, and start to design a model around your curiosity.

You'll know you have built a solid financial Frame when you start being able to connect financial numbers to what they drive — or hinder — for your wider business purpose and goal. Remember, you don't have to be able to fully understand each and every figure on your financial report: if you can see how money is generally flowing, you'll be set up to start focusing in and then, as we'll see later, start engaging in better conversations you're your Finance team. So, with a Frame in your head, you're ready to move onto the next F in our framework — Focus.

# PART THREE

# FOCUS

*"We now accept the fact that learning is a lifelong process of keeping abreast of change. And the most pressing task is to teach people how to learn."*

*– Peter Drucker*

CHAPTER SIX

# What Matters and What Doesn't

In May 2024 the whole city of Wellington erupted in shock thanks to a human error in a budgeting spreadsheet. Over the course of the previous few years, thousands of water pipes had sprung leaks. By the end of the summer of 2024 it had become clear that there were serious problems with deteriorating pipes throughout the city. Hundreds of kilometres of pipes, it turned out, were in extremely poor condition and would need extensive repairs.[1] The recommendation was to replace 40 kilometres of pipe each year, and the council was under pressure to find space in the budget for the project. But the whole situation ended in utter disaster. Out of the 40-kilometre goal, less than a single kilometre of pipe ended up getting replaced — less than a third of what had been completed the year before. On top of that, the city had spent more money than ever before to get the work underway.

The main culprit for everything going so poorly? Everyone was focused on putting effort into the project, not on actually ensuring the outcomes from the project. In other words, all the focus was misplaced by the people making the big decisions.

Dozens of headlines, a damning report, and too many apologies from officials later, an even more frustrating situation emerged: a spreadsheet blunder led to Wellington Water underestimating the project costs by over $50 million.[2] Unsurprisingly, the public was furious. How could something so dramatic go unnoticed? How could they possibly have spent more than ever to return next to nothing?

When I read about this story, so many parts of it felt woefully familiar. In my experience, poor financial decisions almost always come back to focusing on the wrong things. When we talk about budgets and money management, very often the focus gets placed on inputs — how much we expect to spend. Seldom do the conversations shift to what really matters at the end of the day — outcomes.

It's easy to celebrate an investment. Look at politicians, announcing new projects or excitedly proving "progress" by releasing gobsmacking dollar figures allocated to new projects, or CEOs touting "innovation" simply by assigning resources to the next trend. It's far harder — although much better earned — to celebrate achievements. But that's where businesses and goals actually move forward.

In the case of Wellington's pipe disaster, there's plenty to unpack and criticise. More than anything else, though, it's a dramatic reminder of the importance of crucial budgetary understanding — not just from the "numbers guy", but from the decision-makers, the people delivering the work, and all of the leaders involved. It's about misplaced focus and misaligned mindsets.

So, let's not be Wellington Water. Let's instead be the team that doesn't just "have" the numbers, but also understands what they mean in context. To get there, we have to learn the art of *focusing on the right things.*

For most non-financial leaders, the challenge isn't getting *access* to information, it's knowing which information to focus on. In this section, we're going to deep-dive on how to think and engage with information in a way that helps you truly understand and leverage insights from financial reporting.

We'll start by talking about the theory and concepts behind Focus, and I'll show you how to shift between big-picture and small-picture thinking. We'll put on some financial bi-focal glasses and get comfortable with understanding your performance both through looking at the details and contextualising the bigger story. Then, we'll look at how to track and measure progress for your business through the use of key performance indicators (KPIs). We'll explore what makes a good North Star metric, and how to identify the right levers in your role or business that actually move the needle. Finally, it's important that we think about how to shift your perspective, so you start thinking bigger, and lean on your understanding of your business to help drive better collaborations with the Finance team.

You'll come away with practical ways to sharpen your focus, so you can lead more effectively, and drive more meaningful outcomes from every conversation with your Finance team.

## Money isn't the goal

This might make me sound crazy, coming from a CFO, but bear with me: More money is never the true goal. Of course, good businesses should be focusing on generating profit. But a big pile of cash on its own isn't actually what reflects a thriving, sustainable, effective business. Not-for-profits understand this intuitively. The goal for them is to deliver on the mission, and money is the means to do that.

The first hurdle for any leader when it comes to focus is understanding that the power of money is what it allows you to do. This is because good business goals aren't about money; they're about outcomes. Money is just what helps you get there.

The first hurdle for any leader when it comes to focus is understanding that the power of money is what it allows you to do.

Part of the problem is that it can be tempting for business leaders to think about money linearly. They think along the lines of "Our big-picture goal is to make *x* dollars this year." But really that's just half of the job done: they then need to think "What will that money allow me to do or achieve next?" Money is a tool, not a goal in itself. What's more money can be put to work in a range of ways, responding to a range of conditions. I think of money as being like the sea. It comes in, it goes out. Sometimes it's very calm and consistent, and at other times it fluctuates dramatically, such as during a storm. When the tide goes out, we don't have less water; it's simply distributed in a new way.

When we get past arbitrary money-based goals, we start to focus our efforts more effectively. This mindset — this more strategically-placed focus — ends up driving the impacts we care about, and usually leads to making better financial decisions along the way.

For example, let's say a library has a goal of raising $5 million to digitise all of its records, and it comes to me for some advice. Because of the funding structure of the library, it isn't be possible to get the required income to make this happen. So we dig a little deeper about the purpose of this goal. It turns out what the library really cares about is getting more engagement and usership; digital access is just one, albeit major, way it knows can drive more interaction with a wider audience.

Now, instead of the main barrier to its goal being *money*, the focus of the conversation becomes about different routes and strategies to get closer to the *purpose*. We start discussing other ways to drive engagement, thinking critically about which collection will be most helpful and used if it is digitised first. That's not to say that more money wouldn't be helpful or that it wasn't important. But by getting clear about what ultimately matters to the operations, the purpose and the future of the organisation, we are able to have a completely different — and more realistic — conversation about what needs to happen.

So as you start to develop a clear focus, shift away from the question "How can we make more money?", and instead start asking "How do we move towards what we want?"

## Narrowing down on what really matters

*"Your money flows where your attention goes"*
– Mel Robbins

Knowing your true goal comes first. But even with that clarity, it can still be hard to determine which numbers, finances and metrics matter the most. That's where it's important to lean on what I call the "big picture/little picture" connection — the ability to figure out which details reflect the bigger picture, and which ones aren't as relevant.

Think of it like baking a cake. A well-made cake has a lot of inputs — ingredients, recipe, equipment, even the altitude of your city can affect the rise of a sponge! You've baked cakes lots of times, but they keep coming up short. Now you've finally figured out that where you keep going wrong is in that last, crucial stage: finding the right balance between under-cooked and over-cooked. Leave it in the oven too long, and it burns. Bake it at a temperature that is too low, and it fails to rise properly and can be soggy in the middle. To be able to better, and more accurately assess whether it's done, you lean on a few key factors such as smell,

Knowing your true goal comes first. But even with that clarity, it can still be hard to determine which numbers, finances and metrics matter the most.

look, colour, and maybe the classic clean-skewer test. Other pieces of information you have at the time — the temperature of the room, whether the dishes are cleaned yet, or how many eggs you have in your cupboard — don't matter.

So often leaders are distracted by those ancillary pieces of information. They're counting their eggs instead of checking their cake.

An executive director at a higher-education provider said to me that her finance business partner had done a great job of explaining and reconciling a variance. However, it was a $3,000 variance on a $30 million budget, so not overly helpful. What's more, by having been drawn down the path of focusing on that minor variance, it was very easy for the executive director to overlook something more major that was going on. In this case, the issue she really needed to get to grips with was why a number of students were dropping out before completing their courses. By understanding why students drop out could, she could improve the selection of who was accepted into the course in the first place, and thus improve completion rates, which would have a much more material effect than the $3,000 variance.

Focus is about figuring out what matters *most* in the big picture, and then using the most relevant, helpful little-picture information to help you make the best decisions to get you there.

## Applying Focus to your reports

Let's apply this idea to a more high-stakes situation: the story of one of my clients, a healthcare provider who was struggling with their focus.

The business model of the healthcare company depended on a few different revenue streams: it employed nurses who provided care in patients' homes, and it also ran a few aged care homes.

In one of my conversations with a senior leader on the team, he told me how everyone was confused about where to look in their financial reports. They received a ton of data, which often felt overwhelming, and none of it seemed to correlate directly to their roles and responsibilities. So, we took a step back together.

First, with the care homes losing money, we focused on what mattered the most: which was to serve more patients and grow as a business by reducing the losses. Then we determined what was the most critical indicator related to that goal: occupancy, which had the biggest impact on the business as a whole. Vacancies meant lost productivity and opportunity, while more patients meant more revenue for the business and more impact for the community.

Suddenly, the financial reports felt a little less confusing. Because now everyone knew exactly what to look for. Instead of feeling the need to read and synthesise a 40-page report, they could go straight to the metrics they knew mattered the most to their big-picture goals.

Linking your big-picture goals to little-picture details is a simple idea, but I know from experience that it can feel very difficult when you're standing in the middle of the operation. So, when in doubt, just break it down into small, outcome-driven pieces:

- your business's *why*, as we talked about in Chapter 5
- your most important or desired outcome, which is not always financial
- the most strategic route to get there
- the metric, ratio or number that reflects how well you're doing on that route.

With some practice, and some reflection about your business and role, this simple list is one of the best ways to narrow in on your focus — and start weeding out the numbers that matter most. With that in mind, the next chapter will show you how to leverage, track and use the right metrics with the right focus.

CHAPTER SEVEN

# Using metrics to help you focus

Now that you have an understanding of why Focus is so important, let's look at how to actually streamline your view onto the metrics that matter most. This chapter will help you find, use and align the key metrics to your business goals. By the end, you'll have a good sense of what key performance indicators (KPIs) are used for and how to decide on the right ones for your business.

Let's dig in.

## What is a KPI?

A KPI — **key performance indicator** — is a something that you lean on to measure the effectiveness of what you are doing and your progress towards a goal. You've probably come across the term somewhere in your role or organisation, but I'd be surprised if you told me that your whole leadership team is on the same page about what the organisation's KPIs are, why they matter, and how the organisation is leveraging them.

I don't mean to sound sassy (well, maybe a *little* bit sassy). It's just that most organisations don't actually choose, define and use KPIs well. It's one of those terms that gets misused and mismanaged all the time. Which is a real shame, because KPIs are one of the most helpful tools when it comes to Focus, and they are an incredible resource for collaborating more effectively across your teams.

KPIs are easy-to-summarise metrics that should get right to the heart of things. Examples might include such things as average per-visit spend, delivery timeframe, customer adoption, lifetime customer value, etc. It's important to realise, though, that while there are many performance indicators that can be identified for your business, only a small handful should be considered *key* performance indicators. The easiest way to differentiate a KPI from all your other performance indicator metrics is that *a KPI will drive the right actions.* And that's why choosing the right ones is so important.

KPIs are easy-to-summarise metrics that should get right to the heart of things.

This also means that the best KPIs for your business might be different to the KPIs of the business across the street, or even to those of your competitors. They should reflect *your* business goals, purpose and strategy. To identify the best KPIs, it helps to start with the big picture, by looking at the ultimate business metric.

## Start with your North Star Metric

Your **North Star Metric** (NSM) is your master KPI that guides your business towards the goal that matters the most. We've talked about the importance of clarifying your purpose as an organisation; your NSM is one metric that helps you measure and determine whether you're on track.

My own North Star Metric, for example, is the number of referrals I get. That's because it shows me that (a) I'm providing quality service for my current customers, and (b) I'm getting more leads into my pipeline without having to rely on expensive marketing or promotional efforts. With a single metric, I'm able to assess what matters most to me: doing good work and getting more of it.

A good North Star Metric should be:

- customer-centred (value or impact delivered)
- actionable (something that you can influence over time)
- measurable and easy to track
- closely linked to growth or strategy
- hard to game (i.e. can't be easily manipulated)

Examples of bad North Star Metrics would be:

- Website traffic (could be gamed or manipulated in the short term)
- Budget spent (doesn't show whether the spend has been effective).

## Set your KPIs

If your North Star Metric is the destination, your KPIs are your cockpit instruments.

*NSM* = *Compass bearing* → Gives direction

*KPIs* = *Instruments* → Progress updates towards the NSM that highlight how each element of your organisation is performing towards your goals

But here's the important thing: those instruments are only valuable when they are helping you move in the direction to which the compass is pointing you.

For example, a CFO might focus on margins, but if your North Star Metric is customer retention, then margin isn't the thing you should be focusing on. If margin goes up but retention drops, the business is going backwards. Instead, KPIs should be focused on the measures that actually contribute to whether or not you'll achieve your North Star Metric.

If we look at an entity like an airline, we could predict that its North Star Matric has something to do with increasing customer loyalty. It might have an NSM of how many miles are flown per passenger. Those numbers would give the airline a fair reflection of how loyal its customers are. But just tracking that metric won't actually show the airline what it needs to focus on each day, so it will need more tangible KPIs to be able to track how it is progressing towards that North Star. Those could be things like customer satisfaction ratings or the number of customer complaints received.

It's worth noting that your NSMs and KPIs can evolve and change with your business. Especially as you grow or adjust your services, it might be necessary to reconsider what metrics actually reflect what's most important to you right now.

So let's put that into practice. Take a look at your team's or organisation's KPIs or metrics and ask:

- What is your team or organisation's North Star Metric (NSM)?
- What 3 to 5 KPIs genuinely influence your NSM?
- Which KPI, if improved, would most likely shift your NSM?
- What are you currently tracking that doesn't contribute to shifting your NSM?

Then it's time to turn into Jack the Ripper (in a much nicer, less bloody way) and kill those KPIs. Cut any measures that *don't* contribute to the NSM. If you've got any KPIs or measures that live in reports but drive no decisions, get rid of them — they're wasting time and resources and probably distracting you from what's most important.

And remember, my golden rule to identify whether a KPI is valuable is:

- If the KPI moving up or down promotes action, then it is a KPI.
- If it doesn't, then it's not a KPI.

## Performance ≠ Outcomes

Before we move on, let's look at one very common misconception that crops up when leaders set KPIs — understanding what we mean by "performance". *Performance* refers to the results that you can control. *Outcomes*, on the other hand, are the results that you can't control , which often happen thanks to a combination of performance and external factors.

For example, you can't force a customer to buy your product or service, you can only control the number of approaches you make and the number of offers you make. If no one is buying your product or service, it's because either you're not making enough approaches or you're making lousy offers.

I realise that's just a whole lot of words, so let's apply them to a concrete example, say, a government housing agency.

We start by looking at the agency's purpose, which, let's say, is to provide social housing and support to individuals and families across the country, aiming to create thriving communities. At first, it might be easy to think that a good North Star Metric would be the total number of homes built in a year. But, given that so much of the home-building process relies on other organisations and entities (like contractors) and their timelines, the agency doesn't actually have most of the control over that particular KPI. Instead, the agency might consider a NSM around the number of building consents it gets through each year. This part of the process relies on the agency's own internal operations — and it reflects meaningful progress towards its primary goal of creating more public housing.

Remember that in addition to its NSM, the agency would need to use additional KPIs to ensure it is tracking in more granular and specific areas towards its NSM. These might be reviewed more frequently on a weekly or daily basis, and include metrics such as proposals submitted, time to consent the application, and the pipeline for new properties.

When developing your KPIs, you might have a mix of outcome-based measures and performance indicators — the important thing is to make sure at least some of your measures are tracking performance, not just the outcome.

In summary:

- your North Star Metric defines long-term value
- your KPIs should move the NSM
- other performance indicators track the activities within your business which can be used to help move your KPIs forward (e.g. number of invoices, call resolution time).

## What about teams that don't influence the NSM?

While the organisation or function should be driven by the North Star Metric, some teams might not be directly able to influence that, or might find it too abstract at their level. For example, in a business where the North Star Metric is to increase recurring business, the production team might not understand how to contribute towards this metric. So for these teams we use **one metric to measure** (OMTM). This is the one outcome that best represents the value the team is consistently creating, and which also ultimately contributes to the NSM. For the production team in the above business, the one metric that matters might be the percentage of perfect products as a percentage of total production.

### *How to choose an OMTM*

Use this team prompt: "What's the one thing we *can consistently control* that best reflects the value we create, *and* helps the organisation move toward its North Star?"

Brainstorm this with your team, or fellow leaders, and then use the following criteria to determine exactly which metric is right:

- Is it specific to our function?
- Can we measure it without confusion?
- Would improving it support the bigger picture?

As an expert in your area, you can play a major role in helping the Finance team understand what the issue really is, how important it is, and how to shift the reporting from what's reportable to what's relevant.

The best way to leverage your financial numbers is to combine them with tangible, action-oriented insights and plans.

The best way to leverage your financial numbers is to combine them with tangible, action-oriented insights and plans. And the best way to know whether those plans and strategies are working is by using aligned, measurable metrics and KPIs.

Tailor your metrics. Make sure you understand how your numbers relate to actual actions and performance. And don't be afraid to zoom in on just the stuff that drives your organisation's bottom line.

## CHAPTER EIGHT

# The Focus Filter

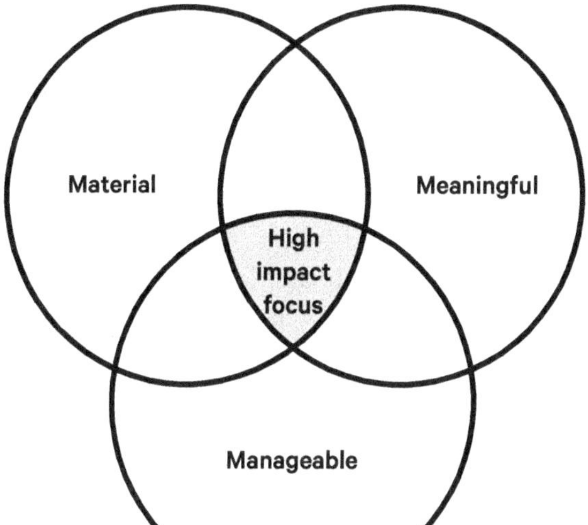


While your North Star Metric is a fantastic way to ensure that you are continuously tracking your progress towards your most important business goals, it's not a catch-all for the process of strategic decision-making. Every day, new challenges and fires pop up in an organisation (though I'm sure I don't have to tell you that!) So when problems present themselves, how do you focus on the right opportunities in front of you to solve them? How do you differentiate the solutions from the just-another-wheel-spinning ideas? That's where I like to bring out my secret weapon: The Focus Filter.

Say you have just received your monthly financial report alongside your KPI and NSM tracking update. You start to review the numbers and you notice something confusing: you seem to be right on track with your all of your identified KPIs and your NSM, and yet your revenue is down.

You scratch your head, thinking "Shoot! Is this a problem with our NSM, our operations, or some other spanner in the works that is affecting our overall financial health?" You call a meeting with your colleagues and start to put together some insights, potential solutions, and areas that you could look at changing or investing in to drive more revenue. Pretty soon, you have quite a few options in front of you, and lots of moving parts, shifting ideas, and proposed goals. Now all you have to figure out is which one to focus on ...

That's where The Focus Filter can help. The Focus Filter helps you to quickly identify where to place your energy and resources. To use it, you simply ask yourself three questions about the potential idea, goal or solution you're considering investing in:

1. Is it material?
2. Is it meaningful?
3. Is it manageable?

Let's now look at these in turn.

## The three core questions

### *Is it material?*

Is it material: does this move the needle either financially or strategically? For example, if the identified issue were to get better or worse, would the organisation move from loss to surplus or surplus to loss?

In accounting terms, *materiality* is described as something that could be reasonably expected to change the economic decisions of someone who might rely on the financial statements. For example, investors to invest, lenders to lend, or grants to be granted.

Depending on what level you are in an organisation (for example, cost or profit centre, business group, division, or group), materiality could mean different things. Something that is immaterial at the division or group level could be material for your cost or profit centre.

Depending on what level you are in an organisation, materiality could mean different things.

Here's how to identify whether something is material:

- If we got this right (or wrong), how big is the impact?
- Would it show up on a dashboard or in a financial report?
- Does it affect revenue, cost, risk, customers or reputation?

Watch out for:

- noise — minor variances and low-value tasks, and
- distractions from "interesting" data that isn't business-critical.

### *Is it meaningful?*

Does it matter to the team or the organisation? For example, an aged care provider schedules its nurses and care workers based on the patients' needs. From the residents' point of view more nurses and care workers equate to better care, but the aged care provider can only charge for the time that has been assessed as needed by the resident. Nurses and care workers are more concerned about the care that they provide than they are about whether the organisation recovers its costs. So here we see a disconnect between the organisation's needs (to run a cost-effective business) and those of the carers and residents (to give and receive optimal care).

If you're a leader where there is potential for a disconnect between organisational needs and what matters to the team and/or the customers, then it is key to make sure that the two sets of needs are connected as any disconnect could potentially be an endless cause of friction and losses.

Here are a few questions to help you judge if the issue is meaningful:

- Does it affect customers, team members or stakeholders directly?

- Is it aligned with the organisation's values, strategy or purpose?
- Will people care about this in three months' time?

Watch out for:

- metrics no one owns, and
- internal distractions ("Initiative du jour") that may feel urgent right now, but won't matter in a few weeks/months.

### *Is it manageable?*

There's little point spending time or energy on things that you can't actually change, so it's vital that you consider whether you can actually do something about the issue that has arisen. For example, where costs have been allocated from head office or you are charged rent or depreciation, then you can't do much about it in the short term. Manageability should also consider what kind of timing is realistic.

Here are some questions to ask that might help clarify the situation:

- Is this within our control or sphere of influence today?
- Can we take meaningful action in the next 30–90 days to improve this?
- Do we have the people, budget or authority to change this over *the next year*?

Watch out for:

- worrying about the things you can't control (e.g. interest rates, inflation, legacy systems), and
- escalating issues instead of acting.

### *Quick diagnostic*

If you're presented with a few opportunities here's how to prioritise the issue or opportunity. Ask yourself and your team the following questions and assign a value:

- How material is this? (0 = no impact, 3 = high financial/strategic impact)
- How meaningful is this? (0 = no one cares, 3 = high stakeholder relevance)
- How manageable is this? (0 = out of our hands, 3 = fully within our control)

Out of a total of 9:

- 0–3: Low focus priority — most likely a distraction
- 4–6: Medium focus priority — consider whether now is the right time to address it
- 7–9: High focus priority — this is what you should be focusing on.

Let's look at an example:

> The issue is that students are dropping out before they complete a course.
>
> - Is it material? Yes, it leads to refunds/lost revenue and wastes a place on the course (3/3)
> - Is it meaningful? Yes, executives and teaching staff care deeply about non-completions (3/3)
> - Is it manageable? Somewhat — we can look at the data and understand why students are not completing the course (2/3)
>
> Total = 8/9. This is where we should be focusing this month!

## Putting it all into practice

So you've learned about North Star Metrics, KPIs, OMTMs and The Focus Filter — now it's time to take it from the theoretical to the real world. Let's take a step back and try to apply all of what we've learned in this Focus step to a case study to show how you could put these ideas into action for your next leadership meeting.

### *Task and context*

Imagine you're a senior leader at an imaginary supermarket chain selling products in-store and online, and you have been asked to choose KPIs for the business.

In general, the primary focus of supermarkets is on increasing their sales revenue, which they can do by either (a) having more customers or (b) encouraging larger purchases per visit. There are probably some other opportunities around efficiency or staffing, but my guess would be that these priorities would be secondary to driving higher sales.

### *Initial response*

Right off the bat, there are a few potential measures I'm starting to see:

- basket value (i.e. bigger purchases)
- weekly traffic (i.e. customers through the door)
- lifetime customer value
- checkout wait times
- return customer visits/loyalty.

However, before you can choose your KPIs, remember first you need to choose your North Star Metric.

### *Narrowing it down to what really matters*

For now, let's assume that your overall goal is to increase the average amount of spend per customer. From that perspective, weekly traffic likely isn't the most direct or useful metric to choose. It doesn't explicitly mean higher profits, and it doesn't factor in long-term sales growth. Similarly, checkout wait times, while they might improve the customer experience, don't directly reflect a shift in sales revenue.

I'd normally be drawn to something like lifetime customer value as the North Star Metric. However, lifetime customer value only works if you can track the individual spend by customer, through something like loyalty cards, as the high lifetime value would reflect really strong loyalty and satisfaction, as well as considering sales.

### *Testing and confirming the North Star Metric*

Let's run that potential metric through the elements we should be looking for:

- Is it measurable?
- Is it easy to track?
- Does it have no upper limit?

In the case of a supermarket, which would likely have a lot of loyalty data available, it's easy enough to track, and it can be measured by dividing the total sales by the number of individual transactions. It passes the no upper-limit test too, allowing for infinite growth and future goals.

Great — so your North Star Metric is *lifetime customer value.*

### *Assigning some KPIs*

Once you're clear on your North Star Metric, you can start to consider what kind of KPIs would be useful, keeping in mind that good KPIs will be things that you can influence and which contribute towards moving the North Star Metric.

Some useful KPIs for this North Star Metric could be:

- wait times at checkouts (as that could impact basket size, due to people having less time to shop)
- the number of customers visiting the store (tracked by sensors on the doors)
- the impact of advertising (measured by the number of items sold which are on special or the number of items in the basket)
- online orders completed versus started (as you could look for ways to get more people to complete their orders to increase value).

### *Identifying an OMTM*

How about for teams who can't contribute to those KPIs, such as the team that unpacks inward goods in the warehouse at each store, or the team that stacks shelves? That's where you'll need to decide on your One Metric to Measure (OMTM). For the inward goods team, it might be the speed to unload incoming goods, place them in allocated bulk areas, and enter them into the data system; perhaps for the shelf-stacking team it would be speed to restock shelves, or something similar that could contribute to always having stock on the shelves for people to buy.

### *Applying The Focus Filter*

Going through this process, although it's all about numbers, it really isn't anything like maths. There is no singular formula or way to get to a "right" answer, which is why it's so important to have the input of strategic-minded, non-financial leaders like you into financial conversations. Remember that you know your business — that is, how it works, what you're working towards, and how you get there — better than the Finance team does. Having both big-picture and small-picture perspective can make you nimble at prioritising issues and assessing solutions.

So let's say you are in a meeting with the Finance team where a discrepancy in the numbers is brought up that doesn't relate to any of your KPIs: a massive increase in the cost of power for the stores.

To decide how much focus to put on it, you'll need to run the issue through The Focus Filter and assign a priority score of from 1 to 3:

- How *material* is this? It increases our expenses significantly but doesn't impact the day-to-day running of the store (2/3)
- How *meaningful* is this? It only matters to those of us who are worried about the bottom line (1/3)
- How *manageable* is this? It is not totally in our control, but we could look to negotiate with our power suppliers (2/3)

Total = 5/9

This makes the issue a medium priority. So instead of redirecting time and resources to it straight away, you might decide to wait and see whether the increased prices continue for another month or two or whether this month's increase is simply a temporary blip. That is, see whether the problem solves itself.

## Conclusion: the value of Focus

Most Finance teams don't have the insight you do about what really matters. Instead they try to second-guess what is important, which means they invariably end up focusing on the symptoms, rather than the underlying problems. By using your North Star Metric, KPIs, OMTM and Focus Filter, you'll be able to get below the surface to see what's really going on and important. (After all, the *Titanic* was damaged by the iceberg below the waterline, not above it!)

# PART FOUR

# FLOW

*Better questions create better outcomes.*

CHAPTER NINE

# Closing the Gap Between Words and Numbers

Shortly after President John F. Kennedy assumed office in January 1961, he was asked to approve a plan to train Cuban exiles to invade Cuba and overthrow Fidel Castro's communist government, with the expectation of sparking an uprising. Advisors thought success stood at 25–30%.[1] But that's not what went into the briefing, which said there was a "fair chance" of success. The implication was that there was a very positive likelihood of success, and consequently approval was given for the "Bay of Pigs" plan to go ahead. The operation turned out to be a disaster. Four American soldiers and 118 Cuban exiles were killed, and 360 wounded. Two B-26 bombers were shot down, and two supply ships were lost during the operation.[2]

Language is ambiguous. Numbers are not. And the translation between them can get messy. A major reason for this is that those who speak with words often think and communicate differently from those who speak in numbers. If you need proof, just think about how many challenging, cyclical conversations you've been part of between budget holders and the Finance team …

> "What does this number mean?"
>
> "This number relates to this other number."
>
> "Okay, and what does *that* number mean?"
>
> "It's an indicator of a different number."
>
> "Can you just tell me what I need to know?"
>
> "I don't know what you're looking for."
>
> "I'm lost."
>
> "Me, too."

You get the picture. Maybe the consequences of these kinds of conversations aren't Bay of Pigs bad, but they can still be incredibly detrimental for your business.

So, what can we do about it?

By following along through the first two Fs — Frame and Focus — you've already built up a solid foundation around understanding how money moves through your business, and how to identify which elements are the most important to focus on. That's a great start to fixing this baseline communication gap.

But now it's time to actually put that understanding into practice. We do that with our third and final "F" — Flow. Flow is when you *flow* all of your new understanding into action. It's learning how to collaborate, ask better questions, and achieve smooth communication and insight-sharing.

There are a few components of Flow that we'll cover in the coming chapters. First we'll look more closely at the gap between numbers and words, and try to get clear on how we can be better translators. Then we'll consider the role our mindset plays in how we collaborate and communicate. And finally we'll learn about the power of questions, and what we can do to think about and ask deeper, stronger questions to drive more effective conversations. Together — by learning to translate, open ourselves up, and ask questions — we will have created a healthy system of flowing with the Finance team.

## Diversity in thinking is a good thing

Before we dive into how to create Flow between departments, it's vital that we understand *why* it's so important that we can collaborate between departments.

In *The Anatomy of a Breakthrough*, Adam Alter explores how individuals and organisations can overcome roadblocks by exploring new perspectives and combining diverse fields of expertise. He highlights the importance of stepping outside one's own field of expertise in order to gain new insights. When experts from different disciplines collaborate, they each bring unique perspectives and methodologies that can shed light on problems in novel ways.

By way of example, let's see how input from people with different strengths could help Emma and her business, Emma's Coffee Shop.

> Emma's creativity, knowledge of coffee, and passion for her community make her a fantastic business owner. She

> thrives with customer communications, inspiring her staff, and devising delicious new scone recipes. However, those strengths don't necessarily translate to thinking in number-terms. She might struggle to synthesise information that comes in the form of statistics, percentages, margins and decimals.
>
> However, it so happens that her business partner has a numbers brain, but isn't nearly as good as Emma is with people, identifying opportunities, and cultivating a coffee-shop culture. Combined, their different strengths make for a good business brain!

Remember, the goal isn't to encourage all non-financial leaders to learn numbers, but to carve out more effective ways for everyone on the team to work together — and not just because they have to, but because it genuinely leads to better results.

Put a number of people with different experiences, skills and expertise in a room to address a problem and their unique perspectives are likely to reveal new paths forward. Then you've got the creativity that comes from being exposed to multiple teams. (And because Finance teams support the whole organisation, they have just this opportunity to mix with colleagues with a diverse range of views and experiences.

Put a number of people with different experiences, skills and expertise in a room to address a problem and their unique perspectives are likely to reveal new paths forward.

This organisation-wide interaction places those in Finance in an ideal position to spot concepts or ideas that one team is using that could also be usefully applied elsewhere in the organisation.)

This ability to share ideas and see problems in new ways drives innovation, and cross-disciplinary work can lead to some breakthroughs that just wouldn't be possible if everyone was keeping to their own silos.

But to get those benefits, you first have to understand each other. You have to be able to communicate. And you have to bridge the gap between your expertise and theirs.

## The words/numbers divide

For those outside Finance teams, words are the go-to. We think we have a good idea of what words mean, and how to use them to get our message across.

But they don't always work the way we want them to, and there's also far too much potential room in them for individual interpretation to be able to ensure clarity and that messages are received as intended.

A particular problem we're likely to encounter in the business world is when "hedging" language is used. If you were to say "I can *confidently predict* that Wellington, New Zealand, *may* experience a *significant* earthquake tomorrow", you wouldn't be wrong. Wellington sits on an earthquake fault and is well overdue in its historical cycle of major quakes. You might even convince someone that an earthquake *will* happen tomorrow. But words like "may" or "could" give flexibility and add ambiguity. Here, you can claim foresight: if the earthquake doesn't happen, you weren't wrong; if it does, you can claim to be psychic. You said it "may" happen, and that is true. Language like this creates ambiguity while also dodging accountability.

Even when words are accurate, you might end up with the wrong result.

Even when words are accurate, you might end up with the wrong result. For example, on 15 October 1987, UK weather forecaster Micheal Fish famously said during a live segment that a "woman had called the BBC and said they'd heard that there was a hurricane on the way. Well if you're watching, don't worry, there isn't." What arrived hours later, however, was the worst storm since 1803.[3]

This was seen as a massive gaffe, but Fish would later defend himself. He was right: a hurricane was not on the way, and he did predict severe weather for the UK. (A hurricane forms in the tropics, while the violent cyclone that hit was classed as "extratropical".) I don't think this "well, actually ..." from Fish made a whopping difference. What people understood — even if it wasn't exactly what he said — was that there was no kind of threat approaching. The preciseness of words can be as unclear as hedging language.

While language is prone to this kind of clear-unclarity, numbers are, by their nature, more objective. Today, my Apple watch can tell me that there's an 80% chance of rain between 7 a.m. and 8 a.m. tomorrow — that's far more accurate and more reliable than any predictions from UK forecasters, who from memory were wrong about as often as they were right! We are much better informed when we have percentages or numbers, whereas we can't quantify feelings. Which means we may choose to leave the umbrella behind when we know there's a 20% chance of rain, but are less likely to if the weather forecast has said there is "a good chance" of rain.

This gap in meaning between words and numbers has been well studied. For example, in 1986 a group of researchers published a paper on measuring the vague meanings of probability terms.[4] In this study, they tackled a simple yet profound question: How do we understand vague terms like "likely" or "probable"? The results showed that our interpretations of probability terms can vary dramatically from one individual to another: One person might think "likely" means 60%, whereas another sees it as 80%. The researchers used a clever method to quantify these interpretations, creating what they called "membership functions", to help map out how different people assign percentages to terms like "doubtful" or "certain". The results were eye-opening: common terms can mean very different things depending on who you ask. This variability in responses affects how we communicate risks and probabilities in everyday life. Herein lies the crux of the problem: words are more open to interpretation than numbers.

It's no wonder, then, that Finance teams love cold, hard numbers. They bring structure, discipline and accountability to conversations. While numbers aren't immune to manipulation or misunderstanding, as we have seen, they are at least clear and more objective. You can't say that something's "mostly 75%" — either it's 75% or it's not. There might be a margin of error in that the percentage, but that's a different story, and is usually noted off to the side. Numbers are precise. But for those who speak in words, understanding numbers can be a step too far — and Finance teams might not be helping themselves here.

## Why does it feel like my Finance team is trying to confuse me?

The curse of knowledge — also known as the curse of expertise or the expert's curse — refers to a cognitive bias where individuals with deep or specialised knowledge assume that others share the same level of understanding. Because the expert knows something to be true, or how something works has been part of their worldview for so long, they can't recall a time when they didn't know what they know. Moreover, when experts work in a team with colleagues with similar expertise, it's easy to assume that, because everyone in their world knows the rule or what a definition is, everyone else also knows the same information. It's probably this cognitive bias that, generally speaking, makes Finance teams difficult to work with.

> Experts find it tricky to communicate effectively with non-experts because they forget what it was like to be a novice and struggle to simplify complex concepts.

It is important to note that here the problem lies in the *communication*, rather than in the *content* they are trying to communicate. But it is also important to recognise that the problem is a nuanced one.

Experts find it tricky to communicate effectively with non-experts because they forget what it was like to be a novice and struggle to simplify complex concepts. This phenomenon can lead to an *empathy gap*, where experts find it challenging to relate to novices, resulting in ineffective teaching, coaching or advising.

As a result, three challenges appear for the Finance team (and anyone working with them!):

1. **Communication barriers:** An inability to communicate the meaning of financial data and strategies can lead to misunderstandings and disengagement on behalf of non-financial experts.
2. **Poor decision-making:** The inability to effectively communicate financial insights can also hinder strategic decision-making within an organisation. Non-financial managers may not fully grasp the implications of their decisions due to the lack of clear communication.
3. **Resource allocation:** The curse of expertise can also affect how resources are allocated and how budget holders are supported. Because finance professionals might underestimate the ability of others to understand complex financial models or underestimate the need for detailed explanations, they might over-engineer allocation plans to avoid non-financial leaders getting confused.

It's important to remember that every time you go away from a meeting with the Finance team scratching your head and thinking "Geez, what's their problem?", chances are they're thinking the same about you!

That little back-and-forth from before where you felt like you were talking to a brick wall? Here's how that little conversation went from Finance's perspective:

> "Finance, what does this number mean?"
>
> "That number isn't going to help you on its own. Don't you want to know about this other number?"
>
> "I want to know about another number now."
>
> "But we haven't finished our conversation."
>
> "Can you tell me about *this* number?"
>
> "Another one?"
>
> "Yes."
>
> "I don't understand you."
>
> "Yeah, me neither."

There's always another side to the coin. The trick is remembering that at the end of the day, heads or tails, you're still connected to the same piece of metal worth the same amount of money. With that in mind, it's time to start engaging in conversations that actually move us forward — for the benefit of your business, your collaboration, your Finance team, and your sanity.

CHAPTER TEN

# Being Open to Learning

*"The only true wisdom is knowing you know nothing."*

– Socrates

Go looking for the foundations of Western philosophy, and you'll find Socrates. A Greek philosopher who lived between 470bc and 399bc, Socrates is generally credited as starting the ethical tradition of thought. He also understood the immense value and positive change that can come from using questions better. Socrates used questions and answers to challenge assumptions and expose contradictions, leading to new knowledge and wisdom. Socrates saw his role not as dispensing knowledge but as a facilitator who provides critical thinking through questioning — so if you find finances challenging, treat this as a strength.

The Socratic method, as it's called, uses questions to challenge assumptions and promote wisdom. It's not about being right, but more about getting to the heart of the matter. Socrates underlined the significance of self-questioning as a fundamental part of personal and intellectual growth. His method of questioning aimed to expose contradictions and lead to a deeper understanding and wisdom, making self-questioning an essential tool for achieving a well-examined, meaningful life.

Questions help us move from confusion to clarity, from compliance to collaboration, from passive reporting to shared ownership.

But why am I harping on about some long-dead Greek philosopher? Because applying the Socratic method to your budget conversations can be genuinely game-changing. When you ask better, more intentional questions, you unlock understanding and trust between the Finance team and budget holders. Questions help us move from confusion to clarity, from compliance to collaboration, from passive reporting to shared ownership.

All the best leaders I know ask questions, are curious, and are open to change. Because of this, they tend to be better collaborators, think more critically, and build stronger engagement with their team. However, most leaders do not ask enough questions for various reasons: egocentrism, apathy, overconfidence in their knowledge, fear of appearing incompetent, or even deep shame from feeling insufficiently knowledgeable.

So, how can we overcome these common blocks to allow ourselves, as leaders, to ask better questions and develop more effective conversations?

## The wrong kind of leadership

Conversations between leaders and those in the Finance team can fall apart when power dynamics, organisational culture and unconscious behaviours discourage open questioning and honest dialogue.

On 15 September 2015, the US Environmental Protection Agency (EPA) issued Volkswagen Group a violation notice, accusing the company of using so-called "defeat devices" on its vehicles to cheat emission tests. The EPA found that Volkswagen had intentionally programmed these devices to reduce harmful emissions during laboratory tests, and installed these "defeat devices" on 11 million cars worldwide since 2006.[1]

Apparently, their vehicles were programmed to detect when they were being tested, and would automatically reduce their emissions of nitrogen oxide. The result was that lab tests showed the vehicles as having extremely low emissions — great if you want to position your brand as reducing pollution. But once the vehicles were out of the lab, and on the road, their emissions were much, much higher.

By June 2020, the scandal known as "Dieselgate" had cost the Volkswagen Group US$33 billion in fines, penalties, financial settlements and buyback costs — and potentially more to their reputation.

At the heart of the scandal was then-CEO Martin Winterkorn, who, at time of writing, had had court proceedings against him suspended due to health issues. (Others implicated in the scandal, including the former head of diesel development, the head of drive train electronics, and two others, have received prison time and suspended sentences.)

By all accounts, Winterkorn had an authoritarian leadership style where people were afraid to deliver bad news or challenge decisions. Former executives have described his leadership style as creating a climate of fear. Winterkorn set ambitious goals for Volkswagen, including the goal of becoming the world's largest carmaker. He was also known for abhorring failure, which contributed to a culture where problems were hidden rather than addressed openly. Because Winterkorn ruled with an iron fist, he oversaw an environment where challenging decisions and speaking up were discouraged. This limited the flow of information and the level and quality of debate within the company. And it may have cost them US$33 billion.

It is easy to dismiss the Volkswagen case as extreme, but the underlying behaviour it revealed is more common than many leaders realise. You may not rule with an "iron fist", but if you're unconsciously dominating conversations — especially in areas where you feel less confident, like finance — you may be shutting down valuable input without knowing it. Many leaders may not even realise that they are dominating. This can be especially the case if numbers aren't your strong point, causing you to speak as often as possible so you don't get asked questions you don't know the answer to.

Many leaders may not even realise that they are dominating.

## What's power got to do with it?

Professors from Harvard, Michigan and Duke universities found that when leaders are focused on their own sense of power they can negatively hurt the performance of their teams. This dynamic was tested in a simulation involving people planning an imaginary climb up Mount Everest.[2] The team consisted of specialists, including a professional climber, a doctor and a photographer. Each scored points according to how many of their goals were met.

For each group, the researchers designated a formal leader. In some cases, they created feelings of power by asking the leaders to write about a time when they had held control over others; in other cases, they didn't. In the interactions that followed, the "high-power" leaders who had done the writing exercise dominated the discussion, talking 33% of the time, while the "neutral power" leaders talked almost half as much, at 19%.

As a result, the first group of leaders missed important clues, such as information from the doctor about the oxygen running low, or opportunities raised by the photographer to earn more points if they stayed an extra day at a certain base camp. In those cases, the team also suffered, achieving an average of 59% of the goals in the first group, compared to 76% in the second group. "Even subtle ways of making people feel powerful have powerful effects on behaviour," noted one of the paper's authors.

Your behaviour impacts both the behaviours of others and the outcomes achieved as a result. You may not be a dominant or authoritarian figure like Winterkorn, but how you act as a leader has a huge impact on how much information you get, and can be the difference between someone speaking up when they have an idea or a solution and them staying silent. Clearly this is limiting and not productive. So how do you overcome this?

With questions.

## The power of questions

Asking questions — and being open to the answers — matters. The kinds of questions we ask matter even more. In fact, learning how to ask questions well — and to ask better questions — is the key to effective leadership and in bridging the gap between Finance and non-Finance teams.

As leaders, we ask others for information all of the time. Unlike professions such as law or journalism, where questioning is a trained skill, most leaders and executives have little training in it, so they often overlook the importance of asking the right question. We also don't always get asked the right questions, and the best thing we can do is learn how to distinguish good questioning from bad, and how to use questions for the better.

Years ago, I was in a budget meeting with the chief executive officer (CEO), chief operating officer (COO) and chief information officer (CIO) of the company I worked for. As the finance manager at the time, it was my job to present the technology budget for approval.

Halfway through the meeting, the COO asked: "Can we produce a report that provides more information on ..." My heart sank.

Could we do it? Yes. But it would be a lot of work — at least two to three days, maybe more. And more importantly than the time taken, I couldn't see what benefit this report would bring to the COO. Nowadays, I'd have simply asked why he wanted the information or what he intended to use it for. At the time, though, I simply resigned myself to spending hours producing the information. Fortunately, the CEO thought it was a pointless exercise, too, and asked, "What benefit is that going to give us?" When it became apparent that the report's usefulness would be limited, especially compared to the time taken to prepare it, the request was shelved.

What has stuck with me about this incident is how innocent-sounding questions from leaders can create excessive work if the question comes across as an instruction. That is, if it is not delivered as inviting a considered answer or to open up discussion. While such a delivery can be innocent and unintentional, it's consequences can be significant, in this case creating unnecessary work and removing time and resource from productive work. In other contexts, it can also lead to unethical policies and behaviour.

## Types of questions

There are many different ways of classifying questions. Take these common examples:

- **Introductory questions:** These are basic inquiries like "How are you?" that start a conversation and set a friendly tone
- **Mirror questions:** These tend to follow on from introductory questions, reflecting the previous response

("I'm fine. How are you?") and maintaining the flow of conversation.[3]

- **Follow-up questions:** These questions solicit more information and show active listening. They are compelling because they indicate that the person is listening and cares about the other person's response.
- **Full-switch questions:** These change the topic entirely.[4] These can be useful for steering the conversation in a new direction or introducing new subjects.
- **Closed questions:** These tend to have specific, simple (often one-word) answers, like "Yes", "No" "Blue", "Tuesday", and so on. There's usually not much room for nuance in answering these kinds of questions, which can also lead to their abusive use by introducing bias, manipulation, or rehearsed answers.
- **Open questions:** These questions encourage respondents to elaborate and provide richer, more detailed answers, and are particularly valuable in innovative contexts, where discovering unexpected answers can lead to breakthrough ideas.

## Questions in action

### *Choosing the right questions*

We need a mixture of these question types, and what gets brought to the front will depend on the situation: the type of information sought, and the conversational environment being created. For example, we probably don't need to ask an open question if we want to know what days payroll happens. A full-switch question can be great for catching someone off-guard, but it can also cause conversational whiplash.

### Finessing your use of questions

To ask better questions, pay attention to what is going on in meetings. Are the questions closed or transactional, or do they invite reflection? You may find it helpful to keep a short journal after key conversations, or even record yourself, and then replay the scenario later, deliberately experimenting by substituting different question types to see whether they engender better information flow and exchanges of views. Good information-gathering techniques include: open prompts ("What would success look like?"), clarifying questions ("Can you explain 'on track'?"), cause-and-effect probes ("What's driving that overspend?") and reflective inquiries ("How did that impact your team?").

To ask better questions, pay attention to what is going on in meetings.

### Pausing and considering

Pausing can be your friend here, too. Before speaking, pause long enough to ask yourself what you really want to understand and/or which outcome you hope to influence.

### *Fostering an enquiring culture*

You can also make questioning part of your team's culture, signalling that an attitude of healthy challenge and openness to change is something expected of everyone. Even when you're not in a meeting with Finance, you could ask "What aren't we seeing?" or "What would Finance challenge here?"

Most people don't go to work wanting to do a lousy job; people generally want to do well and to be helpful where they can be. The seeds of collaboration are already there. So instead of both you and the Finance team approaching your discussions as transactional, what if you set out to educate the Finance person and by approaching the conversation with curiosity and use it as an opportunity to educate yourself to improve your understanding and discover areas you could improve?

For that level of thinking and development, we'll need to take a more structured, thoughtful approach to how we conceptualise and construct powerful, probing questions.

CHAPTER ELEVEN

# Asking Better Questions

*"My job has become less about giving answers to problems and more about asking questions."*
– Jensen Huang, cofounder and CEO of technology giant, Nvidia

"What am I looking at?" a budget manager might ask, when the real question should be "Why — or how — does this matter?" While we generally value answers rather than questions, there is nothing more fruitless than the right answer to the wrong question.

We've looked at how and why communication between the Finance team and budget holders often fails — in other words, the typical barriers to healthy Flow in our process. But now, let's look at what we can do to set us out on a stronger route: asking better questions. In this chapter, we'll get into the weeds with what makes a good question, and the theories we can leverage to dig deeper when we ask these questions.

As Socrates pointed out, asking good questions lies at the heart of learning. Educators value questions because questions encourage students to think critically and help them monitor their learning. The power of questions lies in their ability to stimulate thinking, learning and transformation. Budget holders can unlock immense potential in themselves, others and their organisations by harnessing the art of questioning. In the words of Nvidia's CEO Jensen Huang that opened this chapter: "My job has become less about giving answers to problems and more about asking questions."[1]

Studies by Alison Wood Brooks and her colleagues at Harvard Business School have highlighted how asking more questions leads to better rapport and understanding among conversation partners.[2] For instance, in speed-dating scenarios, participants who asked more questions were more likely to secure a second date. This demonstrates that questioning can build rapport and improve interpersonal relationships. The researchers identified that the first step in becoming a better questioner is to ask more questions. The good news is that effective questioning can be learned and practised, so let's look at a few ways you can hone this skill.

## Types and tactics for better questions

Have you ever been in a budget meeting and suddenly had an overwhelming sense of *déjà vu*? The same questions keep getting asked, the same unhelpful responses keep getting stated … This situation might be happening because everyone is asking closed, transactional questions, instead of open, theoretical questions.

Questions like "What's included in this?" and "What makes that up?" and "Why am I overspent?" are transactional. They ask for information — but don't probe for insight. These are what we could consider closed questions (i.e. there's usually only one right answer), and the answers are soon forgotten by the recipient. In fact, I've known budget holders or stakeholders to ask the same question each time we discussed the monthly report!

> Studies have shown that the best learning moment happens when students co-construct knowledge, not when they simply ask questions and get an answer.

Studies have shown that the best learning moment happens when students co-construct knowledge, not when they simply ask questions and get an answer. Budget conversations are the same. Everyone gets way more value through meaningful, thought-provoking discussion rather than just interview-style question-and-response interactions.

## Frameworks for engaging with enquiry

Teachers and academics classify question types based on cognitive demand: in other words, how much they require the person answering the question to think critically. Several frameworks have been devised to identify and guide the most effective ways to teach and learn. While constructed for the educational sector, the theory can be transferred equally well to any field of enquiry and information-seeking. Following is a brief description of two of the most popular, seminal frameworks.

### *Benjamin Bloom's Taxonomy of Educational Objectives*

Benjamin Bloom's *Taxonomy of Educational Objectives* is probably the most recognised system when it comes to classifying questions, so let's take a look at how it works and what we can learn from it.

Bloom's taxonomy categorises questions from lower-order, which focuses on recall and comprehension, to higher-order, which requires analysis, evaluation and creation.[3] Higher-order questions are more effective in enhancing both recall and the application of knowledge. The taxonomy provides a structured framework to help learners progress over time, which aligns well with the need for finance professionals to gain a deeper understanding of concepts, regulations, data analysis, decision-making skills and business partners.

### *Norman Webb's Depth of Knowledge (DoK) framework*

Bloom's taxonomy inspired the development of Dr Norman Webb's Depth of Knowledge (DoK) framework.[4] The DoK framework was designed to align curriculum instruction and assessments with cognitive complexity, and was aimed at cultivating critical thinking skills in students beyond content coverage. Basically: to promote deeper conceptual understanding and application of knowledge rather than just surface-level memorisation.

## The DoK framework in action

For our purposes of asking better questions of the Finance team, we're going to use Webb's DoK. That's because the framework lends itself to designing questions that progressively increase in complexity, which can challenge the Finance team to demonstrate deeper comprehension and apply financial concepts to the organisation's strategy and tactics. Also, because the DoK allows for fluid movement between levels within a task or question, it aligns well with the complex nature of an organisation's financial environment. Financial analysis and decision-making processes require the recalling of information, the application of skills, strategic thinking, and extended reasoning — often all at the same time!

Let's take a look at how it works.

> **Level 1 (Recall):** Asking questions that recall basic facts, provide definitions, or describe policies and procedures related to their work establishes a foundational knowledge base. For example: "*What is the current budget for my department?*"
>
> **Level 2 (Skill/Concept):** Framing questions that require people to solve routine workplace problems or make decisions based on established ways of working or procedures. For example: "*What would the impact be of a 5% budget cut on our department's operations?*"
>
> **Level 3 (Strategic thinking):** Posing questions that demand strategic thinking, reasoning, justification and evidence-based decision-making in complex

environments. For example, *"What are the pros and cons of different cost-cutting strategies, such as hiring freeze, reducing travel expenses, or delaying equipment purchases? What would be a more strategic approach in line with our department's priorities?"*

**Level 4 (Extended thinking):** Asking questions that require Finance team members to synthesise information from various sources, use critical thinking across disciplines, and apply knowledge to new, real-world situations. For example: *"Could you critique the current budget process and suggest new ways we could improve transparency, accountability and stakeholder engagement, drawing best practices from different organisations and industries?"*

Finance teams often default to communicating through numbers and facts. Budget holders, meanwhile, tend to ask questions that are transactional: "Why am I overspent?" or "What's included in this?" These are Level 1 or Level 2 questions in Webb's Depth of Knowledge framework — useful for clarifying facts, but limited in scope. They rarely lead to insight, strategic alignment, or learning.

But imagine if those conversations regularly moved into Level 3 or Level 4 territory, where finance and business leaders ask each other questions like:

- What would happen if we reallocated budget based on forecasted demand rather than historical spend?

- What is the long-term impact of freezing recruitment now?
- Where have we seen similar challenges elsewhere in the organisation, and what worked?

This kind of questioning changes the nature of the Finance team's role from being a reporting function to becoming a thinking partner. It also unlocks more value from the data that Finance works so hard to produce.

## Entering into Flow

Whether you are a budget holder, a people leader or a finance professional, you have the chance to be the person who signals it's okay not to have all the answers — and shows that better questions lead to better outcomes.

Being in a state of Flow should feel easy, natural and seamless. When all of the cogs are working together effectively, when you're asking the right questions, and critically thinking in a way that aligns with Finance, you'll start to notice that decisions become easier to make. You'll gain a deeper sense of awareness about your business. That's the power of understanding and approaching money not just as a scary, annoying block of numbers — but as an ongoing conversation.

Being in a state of Flow should feel easy, natural and seamless.

The final step of this journey is to start taking action. The 3Fs have equipped you with everything you need to identify better opportunities and make more strategic decisions. While a huge part of Flow is learning how to ask better questions, it's important to remember that the value of that process is in the insights, the conversations, and the wider understanding you get from those in your Finance team as a result. With that much larger grasp of your business, your numbers, and how it all fits together, you have what you need to flow into meaningful, strategic action.

When you can bring The 3 Fs together, with a clear Frame of your finances, a sense of where to Focus, and communication that Flows, you'll start to see and understand money in a whole new way. And that's where magic really starts to happen.

CONCLUSION

# Bringing It All Together

*"We now accept the fact that learning is a lifelong process of keeping abreast of change. And the most pressing task is to teach people how to learn."*

– Peter Drucker

Congratulations! You made it to the end of a book about finance without giving up, crying into a spreadsheet, or faking a headache. That alone is cause for celebration. But more than that, you've taken a big step. Not toward becoming an accountant (oh, perish the thought!), but toward becoming something far more valuable to your business: a curious, confident and capable leader who can engage with financial matters in a meaningful way. That's what *Money Talks* is all about.

Most finance books assume you want to be part of the numbers club. They speak to you like you are two failed exams away from joining the Institute of Chartered Accountants. But that's not why you're here. You just want to unlock better, more strategic ways to understand and lead in your team — and now you can.

But before you toss this book aside, let's remember what we've covered, why it matters, and what's most important as you move forward with your leadership and your conversations with your Finance team.

## It's not about numbers; it's about knowing what to ask

We began with the biggest myth of them all: that you need to be "good with numbers" to understand finance. That's just not true. So long as you have some basic numeracy skills and a curious mindset, you can get a broad but thorough understanding of how money works, how cash flows, and what it says about how your business is doing.

If you've ever asked "Wait, but *why* is that our target again?" then you already have the kind of critical thinking mindset you need. All I've set out to do is give you a way to structure that curiosity so that it leads somewhere useful.

We've talked about the pitfalls of strictly allocating budgets to different jam jars: while it may have worked well for corralling childhood expenses, it is not so useful for managing dynamic, large organisations. Instead, we started thinking about the money in your business as being stored in a large bucket, with cash flow being the water pouring in and out of it, in turns topping it up and depleting it.

We got super simple: if there's more money coming in than going out, you're in a good position. An empty or leaky bucket is a bad sign. To dig into the deeper complexities and the *way* that cash flows in and out of your bucket, we turned to our trusted framework: The 3 Fs.

*Frame* taught us how to leverage models to visualise and understand the inner workings of how money flows through a business.

*Focus* showed us that not every detail on our financial report is important to each role. We looked at strategies for delineating what's important and what's a distraction, and we covered the process for deciding on a meaningful North Star Metric and useful KPIs.

Finally, *Flow* gave us the tools to actually begin collaborating and communicating with Finance teams. We looked honestly at what often gets in the way of finance thinkers and non-finance thinkers communicating successfully, and at what makes a great question based on educational psychology.

Ultimately, what we created was a simple overview of how to think about finance in a way that doesn't require you to "get" numbers.

## You don't need to speak numbers — you need to embrace curiosity and awareness.

Formula-shormula! Of course formulas, statistics and spreadsheets are essential to good accounting practice. But that doesn't mean you, as a non-financial leader, have to be able to do this all yourself, or even understand how each piece of information is sourced. Instead, the key to nailing The 3 Fs is to see the bigger picture. To understand the general terms, keep your focus on the metrics that reflect your most important business and operational goals, and keep ongoing conversations flowing with the people on your team who *do* know how to leverage the formulas.

As you go forward with your role and your journey to feeling confident talking about money, here are a few of my favourite questions that you can lean on whenever you're finding yourself either too up in the clouds or too down in the branches:

- If we're doing "well", why are we running out of cash?
- What assumptions are we making in this forecast?
- What story are these numbers telling? What story is not being told in these numbers?
- What would we see if we looked at this from a customer's perspective?
- What are we optimising for? Is that still the right goal?
- What does "good" look like, and are we getting closer to it?

If you start asking questions like that — bringing together the valuable perspectives of people across your leadership table — you will undoubtedly see shifts. Your Finance team will start bringing you better data to match the strategic focus areas. Your non-financial leaders will start becoming more open and curious about the kind of data and insights that could help them make better decisions. And, most importantly, you'll start having conversations that continuously and cleverly move you towards the outcomes that matter for the business.

## Finance is a tool for everyone

I hope this book has not just given you a sense of how to approach this scary topic, but it's even made you excited to explore what you could learn and gain by becoming more involved with financial matters.

I truly believe that businesses thrive when financial insights are at the heart of strategic conversations. This isn't to say that the Finance team has all the answers, or should be leading every decision. It's more about opening the door for everyone to see how money reflects, impacts, and tells a story of success. Finance isn't just for numbers people. It's for every leader who wants to make their organisation better, stronger and more aligned.

So, as you go forward in your role, be curious. Be open. Ask questions. Ignore the jargon. And when in doubt, don't *do* the numbers — dig deeper to understand why they're there in the first place.

BONUS CHAPTER

# A Note for Finance Teams

If this book has made one thing clear, it's that non-financial leaders often struggle to connect with and collaborate effectively with those in their Finance teams. And we've talked a lot about what non-financial leaders can do about it — by understanding the basics outside of just looking at numbers, and turning towards The 3 Fs. But now I'd like to offer a small token just for my Finance friends. A word of advice, I suppose, about how you — accountants, financial thinkers, number lovers — can better understand, support and collaborate with your non-financial counterparts.

I'll start by saying that I myself am in fact a numbers guy, a former CFO who now consults with Finance teams to improve their influence. I've spent my career supporting, consulting and helping other finance teams improve how they do things and how they can help make their whole business more effective. So, in essence, although I've written this book for non-financial leaders, I'm actually one of those people who can understand both sides.

One thing I've noticed in my time (which in large part has been a big motivator for writing this book) is that communication is often so full of friction when Finance and non-Finance people get together. That's not something we can just blame one side for, either. People are coming from different backgrounds, with different perspectives, and with widely different understandings and knowledge about their business and their craft. So, whether your non-financial leader just handed you this book and you've flipped to the back here, or you're seeing this after reading through the whole thing, I'd like to share three bits of wisdom that I like to lean on as a Finance guy who spends a lot of time coordinating and communicating with non-Finance people. These are the things I've seen help immensely when it comes to developing stronger relationships, better collaboration, and improving the overall business.

## #1. Take the time to understand what gets in the way

Most Finance teams spend their days knee-deep in — or more accurately trying to keep their head above — operational tasks: reconciling accounts, closing month-end, processing bills, producing reports, and responding to myriad urgent requests. Often these involve trivial policy matters such as "How much can I claim for this?" which could easily be read on the intranet, or fielding questions from suppliers about why they haven't been paid.

Finance teams are busy being busy. It is like battling a nine-headed hydra: cut one down and another grows back. With only so much time in a day, most of the Finance team's time is spent dealing with the urgent. Unfortunately, the important tasks are often dealt with by working longer hours, and, with so little discretionary time available, minimal effort is spent on improving processes, building relationships, or engaging in strategic thinking.

For senior leaders outside of Finance, many interactions with the Finance team are compliance-based — approving items, signing off documents or getting digital templates. Consequently, when a leader's experience is transactional, they are unlikely to think of Finance as a team to help with strategy. Worse, if a senior leader does have a strategic issue where they need the Finance team's assistance, the team is likely too busy with transactional work to provide meaningful help, thus creating a doom loop where the Finance team is seen as neither helpful nor strategic.

In my experience, most people who take a role in the Finance team do so because they want to help and make things better. However, they often only gain satisfaction from reconciling the payroll journal or bank account. As I teach the CFOs I work with, the first step to becoming more influential is to create more capacity. Constant busyness does not allow sufficient time for strategic thinking or relationship-building.

The solution? Let go of the small stuff and focus on activities that create capacity, such as reducing month-end processing times and report production, to create more time for work that matters.

The most common barrier I see is simply too much on CFOs' plates — and too little recognition of what that "operational overload" is doing to their overall effectiveness for the business. So make sure you're carving out time specifically for sitting down, connecting with, and communicating with your non-financial counterparts.

Consider setting up office hours once a week where anyone can swing by your desk and ask all of their questions. Or you could create a standing meeting where you go over the financials and individually check in with each department to make sure they understand what's being said and why it's important to them.

## #2. Try to connect what you're doing with the wider business

The potential for the Finance team to add significant value to any organisation is immense. You are involved in all of the numbers, speak to every department, and have the ability to tell the story of what's going on in the organisation. But therein lies the problem. Once stuck in operational tasks, Finance teams often begin facing criticism for not understanding the business. Understanding the business is crucial for Finance teams to be influential and be able to identify opportunities or risks. While you may know the balance sheet, the profit and loss account, and the budget figures to the last decimal point, it is equally important to understand what drives these numbers — who your customers are and how the product or service is delivered.

In my experience, many Finance teams spend very little time at the coalface or on the shop floor, making it difficult to truly connect the numbers to the relevant activities. Early in my career, I went on a site visit to an operations centre near Heathrow Airport. A few weeks later I saw a payment to a supplier for painting the floor at this warehouse. Even though it was a while ago when costs were lower, I realised you couldn't paint the floor of that particular warehouse for just a few hundred pounds. Connecting this information to my personal experience revealed fraud, resulting in several people losing their jobs, including a business unit general manager who wasn't involved in the fraud.

I think Finance teams simply are not curious enough and don't ask enough "why" questions. Without a deep understanding of the organisation, any insights the Finance team provides are likely to be superficial. The numbers might be accurate, but they won't tell the full story, just like reading the scoreline of an FA Cup semi-final between Manchester City and Nottingham Forest, or an England versus All Blacks rugby test match doesn't tell you whether it was a good or bad game.

## #3. Invest in your own soft skills

I get it: you probably got into this role because you thrive in technical, logical, certain environments. Maybe because of your love of numbers. Numbers are for sure; social interactions, not so much.

But when you get to a certain level — CFO or otherwise — you need to bring more to the table than just your excellent accounting knowledge or your top exam scores. Leadership is more than expertise: it's influencing, inspiring, listening, storytelling and relationship-building. And if you aren't thriving in those areas, it's time that you start putting more effort into them.

If you, as a leader, find these sorts of skills challenging and don't understand your organisation's value drivers beyond a technical level, how can you expect your people to do so? Technical expertise impresses other accountants, not senior leaders looking for practical solutions. Throughout my career, I can genuinely think of only a handful of situations requiring deep technical accounting expertise, and even then it was cheaper to outsource.

Great Finance team leaders don't just close the books; they teach their team how to turn data into stories and connect the dots to inspire action. Finance team leaders need to identify and develop those with a natural affinity for building relationships and asking good questions.

A major part of an effective CFO's role is helping others understand finance and assisting them, but this requires you to not only have the capacity for conversations like that (remember the first point in this series?), but to also have the social and personal skills and patience to hold a safe and effective space for those dialogues.

If you read through the book up until this chapter, you'll be familiar by now with the kinds of questions I encouraged non-financial leaders to bring to you, their top financial thinkers. *Now, it's your turn to meet them where they're at.* This is about providing thoughtful, clear and kind answers. Sometimes, you might feel like their question doesn't make sense; if you can work out what they actually intend to say or ask, try to explain the discrepancy and give them the insights you suspect they're looking for. Remember that good conversations — conversations that actually move the needle — are about helping everyone make better decisions for the business. Try to keep the overall outcomes and the real-impact insights at the top of your mind. I promise it won't just be your non-financial leaders who benefit — you'll also start noticing smarter decisions being made, easier (less frustrating!)

questions and issues coming your way, and improved awareness throughout your team.

## A final note

The goal for everyone is to create a joint understanding of priorities. Master your collaboration between the Finance team and other teams and you'll start to see the benefits of an organisation that has everyone operating on the same page.

Don't forget your worth: the powerful perspective you have that comes from having visibility across the whole business. When others come to you with misunderstandings or questions that might not at first make sense, try to bring to them the powerful perspective you have. The results could truly transform the way you work.

# Endnotes

## Introduction

1. Bergstrom, Carl, & West, Jevin. (2021). Calling bullshit: The art of scepticism in a data-driven world. Penguin.
2. Lallanilla, Marc. (2014, April 23). Misleading gun-death chart draws fire. Live Science. https://www.livescience.com/45083-misleading-gun-death-chart.html
3. Satherley, Dan. (2020, January 30). National Party's "mischievous" bar graph cleared by advertising watchdog. Stuff. https://www.stuff.co.nz/politics/350529535/national-party-s-mischievous-bar-graph-cleared-by-advertising-watchdog
4. Fine, Benjamin. (1956, June 4). Teachers chided on mathematics. The New York Times. https://www.nytimes.com/1956/06/04/archives/teachers-chided-on-mathematics-study-finds-them-deficient.html

## Chapter One: The Basics

1. The terms 'organisation', 'business', 'function' and 'area' are used throughout this book, often interchangeably. However, they do mean slightly different things depending on your role. As a senior leader, you might be interested in the performance of your business group. As the CEO you'd be interested in the performance of your organisation or the business. If you are the team manager you'd be interested in the performance of your team. So as I use the terms (organisation, business, function, area), it's important to adjust

what this means to you depending on your role, perspective and focus area.

2. Hendricks, Drew. (2014, July 7). 5 Successful Companies That Didn't Make a Dollar for 5 Years. Inc.com. https://www.inc.com/drew-hendricks/5-successful-companies-that-didn-8217-t-make-a-dollar-for-5-years.html
3. Hoenig, Henry. (2025, February 24). The history of Uber. Investopedia. https://www.nytimes.com/1956/06/04/archives/teachers-chided-on-mathematics-study-finds-them-deficient.html

## Chapter Six: What Matters and What Doesn't

4. Hunt, Tom. (2025, November 24). Less than 1km of "very poor" Wellington pipes fixed this year. The Post. https://www.thepost.co.nz/nz-news/360497607/less-1km-very-poor-wellington-pipes-fixed-year
5. Vance, Andrea. (2025, March 2). Money down the drain: Scathing Wellington Water report explained. The Post. https://www.thepost.co.nz/nz-news/360599398/money-down-drain-scathing-wellington-water-report-explained

## Chapter Nine: Closing the Gap Between Words and Numbers

1. John F. Kennedy Presidential Library and Museum. (2024, November 7). The Bay of Pigs. https://www.jfklibrary.org/learn/about-jfk/jfk-in-history/the-bay-of-pigs
2. Ibid.
3. Met Office. (n.d.). Lessons and legacy of the Great Storm of 1987. https://www.metoffice.gov.uk/about-us/who-we-are/our-history/lessons-and-legacy-of-the-great-storm-of-1987
4. Wallsten, T. S., Budescu, D. V., Rapoport, A., Zwick, R., & Forsyth, B. (1986). Measuring the vague meanings of probability terms.

Journal of Experimental Psychology: General, 115(4), 348–365. https://doi.org/10.1037//0096-3445.115.4.348

## Chapter Ten: Being Open to Learning

1. United States Environmental Protection Agency. (2015, September 18). VW Notice of Violation, Clean Air Act. https://www.epa.gov/sites/default/files/2015-10/documents/vw-nov-caa-09-18-15.pdf
2. Tost, Leigh Plunkett, Gino, Francesco, & Larrick, Richard P. (2013). When power makes others speechless: the negative impact of leader power on team performance. Academy of Management Journal, 56(5), 1465–1486. https://doi.org/10.5465/amj.2011.0180
3. Brooks, Alison Wood, & John, Leslie K. (2018, May–June). The surprising power of questions: It goes far beyond exchanging information. *Harvard Business Review* https://cebma.org/assets/Uploads/hbr-the-surprising-power-of-questions.pdf
4. Ibid.

## Chapter Eleven: Asking Better Questions

1. Chevallier, A., Dalsace, F., & Barsoux, J.-L. (2024, May 1). The art of asking smarter questions. Harvard Business Review. https://hbr.org/2024/05/the-art-of-asking-smarter-questions
2. Brooks, Alison Wood, & John, Lelie K. (2018). The surprising power of questions: It goes far beyond exchanging information. Harvard Business Review. https://cebma.org/assets/Uploads/hbr-the-surprising-power-of-questions.pdf
3. Bloom, B. S., Engelhart, M. D., Furst, E. J., Hill, W. H., & Krathwohl, D. R. (1956). Taxonomy of educational objectives: The classification of educational goals. Vol. I: Cognitive domain. New York: David McKay Company; Stapleton-Corcoran, Erin. (2023, January 25). Bloom's Taxonomy of Educational Objectives. University of Illinois Chicago. https://teaching.uic.edu/cate-

teaching-guides/syllabus-course-design/blooms-taxonomy-of-educational-objectives/

4. Hess, Karin. (2013). A guide for using Webb's Depth of Knowledge with Common Core State Standards. https://smartlearningsystems.com/wp-content/uploads/2014/10/WebsDepthofKnowledgeFlipChart_nobleeds_05142013_0001.pdf

# Unlock your Money Talks toolkit

To access the set of practical tools I've created to help you put these ideas to work straight away, scan the QR code below, or head to **https://resources.matthewneedham.co/money-talks**, and you'll unlock the companion worksheets, short videos and extra resources.

# Equip your Finance team to influence, not just report

Numbers alone don't drive performance: influence does.

That's why I run **Finance Influence workshops** and **1:1 coaching for CFOs and their teams:** practical, high-impact (and fun!) sessions designed to shift Finance teams from reporting the numbers to shaping decisions.

This is part of **FinanceOS**, my structured programme to help build Finance teams with lasting influence and impact.

To discuss how you can work with me to improve the influence of your Finance team, scan the QR code to book a call.

# Bibliography

Alter, Adam. (2024). Anatomy of a breakthrough. Simon & Schuster.

Bergstrom, Carl, & West, Jevin. (2021). Calling bullshit: The art of scepticism in a data-driven world. Penguin.

Brooks, Alison Wood, & John, Leslie K. (2018, May–June). The surprising power of questions: It goes far beyond exchanging information. Harvard Business Review. https://cebma.org/assets/Uploads/hbr-the-surprising-power-of-questions.pdf

Brown, Brené. (2015). Rising Strong: The reckoning. The rumble. The revolution. Penguin Random House.

Chevallier, Arnaud, Dalsace, Frédéric, & Barsoux, Jean-Loius. (2024, May 1). The art of asking smarter questions. Harvard Business Review. https://hbr.org/2024/05/the-art-of-asking-smarter-questions

Dorsey, Lauren E. (2020, December 4). Trial of Socrates. Ancient World Magazine. https://www.ancientworldmagazine.com/articles/trial-socrates/

Fine, Benjamin. (1956, June 4). Teachers chided on mathematics. The New York Times. https://www.nytimes.com/1956/06/04/archives/teachers-chided-on-mathematics-study-finds-them-deficient.html

Hendricks, Drew. (2014, July 7). 5 Successful Companies That Didn't Make a Dollar for 5 Years. Inc.com. https://www.inc.com/drew-hendricks/5-successful-companies-that-didn-8217-t-make-a-dollar-for-5-years.html

Hess, K. (2013). A guide for using Webb's Depth of Knowledge with Common Core State Standards.https://smartlearningsystems.com/wp-content/uploads/2014/10/WebsDepthofKnowledgeFlipChart_nobleeds_05142013_0001.pdf

Hoenig, Henry. (2025, February 24). The history of Uber. Investopedia. https://www.investopedia.com/articles/personal-finance/111015/story-uber.asp

Hunt, Tom. (2025, November 24). Less than 1km of "very poor" Wellington pipes fixed this year. *The Post*. https://www.thepost.co.nz/nz-news/360497607/less-1km-very-poor-wellington-pipes-fixed-year

John F. Kennedy Presidential Library and Museum. (2024, November 7). *The Bay of Pigs*. https://www.jfklibrary.org/learn/about-jfk/jfk-in-history/the-bay-of-pigs

Lallanilla, Marc. (2014, April 23). Misleading gun-death chart draws fire. *Live Science*. https://www.livescience.com/45083-misleading-gun-death-chart.html

Met Office. (n.d.). *Lessons and legacy of the Great Storm of 1987*. https://www.metoffice.gov.uk/about-us/who-we-are/our-history/lessons-and-legacy-of-the-great-storm-of-1987

Satherley, Dan. (2020, January 30). National Party's "mischievous" bar graph cleared by advertising watchdog. *Stuff*. https://www.stuff.co.nz/politics/350529535/national-party-s-mischievous-bar-graph-cleared-by-advertising-watchdog

Stapleton-Corcoran, Erin. (2023, January 25). *Bloom's Taxonomy of Educational Objectives*. University of Illinois Chicago. https://teaching.uic.edu/cate-teaching-guides/syllabus-course-design/blooms-taxonomy-of-educational-objectives/

Tost, Leigh Plunkett, Gino, Frabcesco, & Larrick, Richard P. (2013). When power makes others speechless: the negative impact of leader power on team performance. *Academy of Management Journal, 56*(5), 1465–1486. https://doi.org/10.5465/amj.2011.0180

United States Environmental Protection Agency. (2015, September 18). *VW Notice of Violation, Clean Air Act*. https://www.epa.gov/sites/default/files/2015-10/documents/vw-nov-caa-09-18-15.pdf

Vance, Andrea. (2025, March 2). Money down the drain: scathing Wellington Water report explained. *The Post*. https://www.

thepost.co.nz/nz-news/360599398/money-down-drain-scathing-wellington-water-report-explained

Wallsten, T. S., Budescu, D. V., Rapoport, A., Zwick, R., & Forsyth, B. (1986). Measuring the vague meanings of probability terms. Journal of Experimental Psychology: General, 115(4), 348–365. https://doi.org/10.1037//0096-3445.115.4.348

# About the author

Matthew Needham is an expert in organisational performance. He is a former award-winning CFO, speaker, consultant, coach, trainer and thought leader. Born in Nottingham, in the United Kingdom, he moved to Wellington, New Zealand, in 2012, before moving across the ditch to Australia in September 2024. He has over 20 years of senior leadership and executive experience working in various sectors, such as aerospace, financial services, telecoms, public sector and not-for-profit organisations. He has run his thought leadership practice since 2023.

He is passionate about helping organisations, leaders and their teams perform better through improved prioritisation and execution, using financial management (and understanding), culture and process improvement.

Matthew lives with his family and two dogs in sunny Sydney. When not delivering workshops or coaching, he can be found standing on the sports-field sidelines cheering on his son in Under-16s rugby, or mountain biking, but more likely walking the dogs.

# Acknowledgements

Well, I've written a book. This is an achievement in itself. Sitting down and doing the work when at times watching paint dry honestly seemed more appealing.

But as Arnold Schwarzenegger says: "I am not a self-made man." So here are my thanks and dedications:

> To my wife Emma, who has been the guinea pig for the ideas and kept me grounded. To my son, Sam, you have inspired me more than you can ever know. Most of all, when you're passionate about something, keep on going. And if you're not inspired, watch TikToks.

www.ingramcontent.com/pod-product-compliance
Lightning Source LLC
LaVergne TN
LVHW052326200926
848481LV00002B/685
* 9 7 8 1 7 6 4 3 2 2 8 0 5 *